I am a Tear of Joy and Sorrow

The story of Masha Wolfsthal

JewishGen
מרכז עולמי לגנאלוגיה יהודית
The Global Home for Jewish Genealogy

A Publication of JewishGen, INC
Edmond J. Safra Plaza, 36 Battery Place, New York, NY 10280
646.494.5972 | info@JewishGen.org | www.jewishgen.org

MUSEUM OF
JEWISH HERITAGE
A LIVING MEMORIAL
TO THE HOLOCAUST

I am a Tear of Joy and Sorrow

The original book was published by the family of Masha Wolfsthal with the kind support of the Holocaust Survivors' Memoirs Project of Yad Vashem, the World Holocaust Remembrance Center.

The book is based on Masha Wolfsthal's story as told to Nava Gibori.
Writing and editing: Nava Gibori.
English Translation: Yotam Wolfsthal.
Design and production: Nurit Pagi.
Cover Design: Rachel Kolokoff Hopper.
Artwork on front cover © Ori Beanstock, with permission of the artist.
Portrait photo on back cover © Martin Schoeller, courtesy of Yad Vashem.

Printed in the United States of America by Lightning Source, Inc.

Library of Congress Control Number (LCCN): 2021949993

ISBN: 978-1-954176-25-6 (hard cover: 194 pages, alk. paper)

About JewishGen.org

JewishGen, an affiliate of the Museum of Jewish Heritage - A Living Memorial to the Holocaust, serves as the global home for Jewish genealogy.

Featuring unparalleled access to 30+ million records, it offers unique search tools, along with opportunities for researchers to connect with others who share similar interests. Award winning resources such as the Family Finder, Discussion Groups, and ViewMate, are relied upon by thousands each day.

In addition, JewishGen's extensive informational, educational, and historical offerings, such as the Jewish Communities Database, Yizkor Book translations, InfoFiles, Family Tree of the Jewish People, and KehilaLinks, provide critical insights, first-hand accounts, and context about Jewish communal and familial life throughout the world.

Offered as a free resource, JewishGen.org has facilitated thousands of family connections and success stories and is currently engaged in an intensive expansion effort that will bring many more records, tools, and resources to its collections.

Please visit https://www.jewishgen.org/ to learn more.

Executive Director: Avraham Groll

About the JewishGen Press

JewishGen Press (formerly the Yizkor Books-in-Print Project) is the publishing division of JewishGen.org and provides a venue for the publication of non-fiction books pertaining to Jewish genealogy, history, culture, and heritage.

In addition to the Yizkor Book category, publications in the Other Non-Fiction category include Shoah memoirs and research, genealogical research, collections of genealogical and historical materials, biographies, diaries and letters, studies of Jewish experience and cultural life in the past, academic theses, and other books of interest to the Jewish community.

Director of JewishGen Press: Joel Alpert
Managing Editor: Jessica Feinstein
Publications Manager: Susan Rosin

I am a Tear of Joy and Sorrow

The story of Masha Wolfsthal

Dedicated with love to the memory of my dear husband Yehezkel
and all members of my family who perished in the Holocaust

This book was published by the family of Masha Wolfsthal
with the kind support of the Holocaust Survivors' Memoirs Project of Yad
Vashem, the World Holocaust Remembrance Center

יד ושם 𐤔
YAD VASHEM
THE WORLD HOLOCAUST
REMEMBRANCE CENTER

English Translation: Yotam Wolfsthal

The book is based on Masha Wolfsthal's story as told to Nava Gibori

Writing and editing: Nava Gibori

Design and production: Nurit Pagi

This English translation of the original book is
lovingly dedicated to my dearest Savta[1] Masha,
living proof of the power of the human spirit, who
rose from incomprehensible tragedy to become a
beacon of hope, purity, light, optimism, strength,
and love in a world filled with adversity,
a believer in the good of people, and the kindest
and most gracious person I know.

Yotam Wolfsthal

———————

תרגום אנגלי זה של הספר "אני זואה של אושר ותקווה"
מוקדש באהבה לסבתי מאשה היקרה לי מכל, שׂשׂרדה
אסון בל יתואר, והתאוששות נפש בלתי-נתפסות הפכה
לראות מופת ולסמל של אור, אהבה, טוהר, תקווה,
אופטימיות ואומץ בעולם שכולו מהמורות וקשיים,
ולאדם האדיב והנדיב ביותר שהכרתי בחיי.

יותם וולפסטל

———————————————

Father's Will:
You need to live, and you will live!

If Father can see me now

If he is watching me from above –

his pride in me is as great as can be!

I am alive!

I remember, I never forgot, I live!

And the chain of the generations will continue!

My dear children,

The memories of the past are a part of me. A part of who I am. Sometimes they appear before me as images from a peaceful time long ago, of growing up in a loving, stable home. Other times, as visions from a childhood abruptly cut short, of a collapsed society in a world shattered without warning. But I always return to the good of the present, to all of you, to life with my family, here, in this land.

In the winter of 2006, I joined my dear grandson Yoad and his entire grade on their school trip to Poland for the March for the Living[2]. For eight days we were there. For eight wintry days I searched my country of birth for the sights and sounds that made up the backdrop of my childhood; for any traces I might have left there. Through the windows of the bus I could see frozen lakes, soaring trees, wild geese tearing through the skies, and white snow stretching as far as the eye can see.

The bus passed by countless signs of villages and towns I knew from my past. I knew Jews used to live in them long ago.

My thoughts took me to my hometown of Kamin-Kashyrskyi in the Volyn Oblast, which no force in the world could ever erase from my memory.

Seeing the glare of the bright, white snow, I remembered the slippery hills, the small wooden slide with which I used to go down the slopes, and the sounds of laughter and joy which punctuated that time of my life.

For a moment, I even thought I could hear someone calling my name… Mashinka … Mashinka …

But no.

Poland of today is a completely foreign land to me. There is nothing on its soil which I hold dear, nothing I miss, not a trace of the countless images I carry within me from the Poland of yore. The only thing left from it is my will to tell my story.

---

[2] The International March of the Living is an annual educational program bringing individuals from around the world to Poland and Israel to study the history of the Holocaust.

My memories, it seems, hold within them the story of the Jewish fate throughout history. I was born into an intimate Jewish community that dreamed of Zionism and of a national revival in the Land of Israel. I had an open, carefree, free-flowing childhood in a mesmeric world.

I experienced the collapse of the world around me, of humanity, and was forced to constantly fight for my life. My eyes saw so much death and cried so many tears.

But after all that, I was bestowed with a wondrous miracle. I was blessed with a long life, found my way back into the human tapestry of the world, started a family and built a home with Yehezkel, and have had the fortune of being here with all of you, filled with joy despite everything I have been through.

Now I wish to gather up all the memories and stories and pass them on to you for posterity.

Stories of both my personal past and that of the world, from another time and place, of people I have loved and will forever remember. Stories I must remember, for all of you.

Because I am the bridge connecting generations past to generations to come. And I feel honored and grateful with every fiber of my being for the opportunity to be that bridge.

My family, my children, my grandchildren, and my dear husband Yehezkel who is no longer with us, thank you for the blissful life we have created here together with so much love.

Mom

A Little Girl Walks Alone in the Woods

A little girl walks alone in the woods.
Trees around her tall and wide, in the great blackness of night.
It is near the end of fall
and the cold of the Eastern-European night permeates the bones.
A reign of darkness rules the world
A chilling, sinister darkness, spreading chaos all around…
The wind brushes past the trees' large leaves and they rustle
asking the girl with a whisper, or perhaps a whistle
"Little girl, are you not cold?"
"Father gave me his big jacket to keep me warm."
"And where is Father now?"
"Left many days ago to search for my brothers and Mother, left and hasn't returned…"
"And your brothers and Mother, where are they?"
"Back in the ghetto they stayed. Escaped perhaps. Or have already died."
"Little girl, you have been left alone in the forest… Are you not afraid?"
"I am very much afraid.
But I do not walk alone.
Walking with me are the words of Father, repeatedly telling me I must live.
Walking with me is the memory of the dream about my dearest grandmother
who told me she would watch over me from above.
And the hope that I will meet good people yet, however few
that will help me continue along…"

A little girl crossed a forest of terrible darkness,
and became a little woman, brimming with wisdom, love, and warmth.
A father's request of life, an assuring dream from Grandma, a small flame of hope
became a wondrous miracle
shining the light of life amidst the endless darkness of hate,
and at the end of the day, love prevailed.

Originally written by Dr. Yoav Shomer, inspired by the survival story of Masha Wolfsthal.

Table of Contents

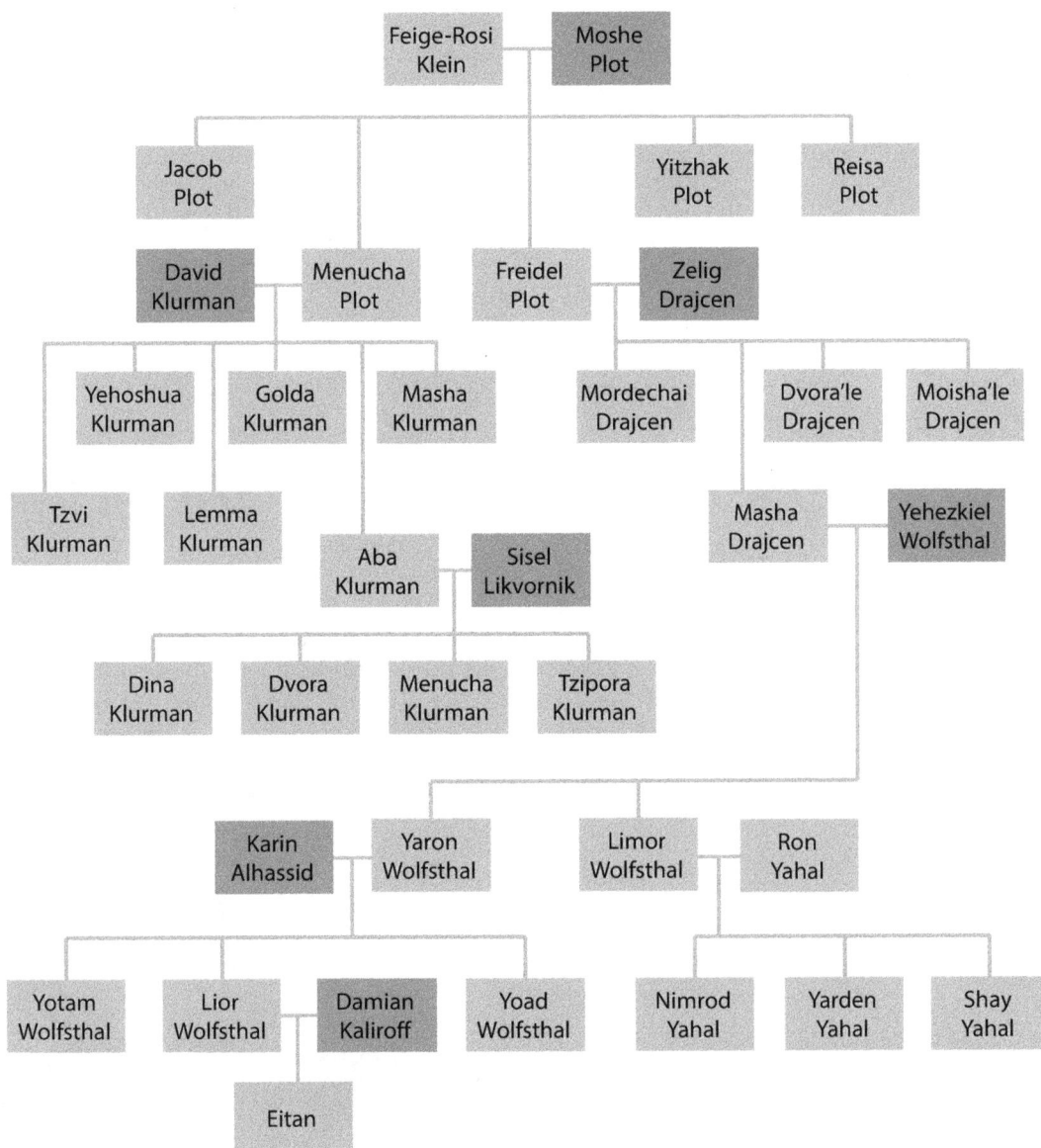

Family Tree

Feige-Rosi Klein — Moshe Plot

- Jacob Plot
- Yitzhak Plot
- Reisa Plot

David Klurman — Menucha Plot

Freidel Plot — Zelig Drajcen

- Yehoshua Klurman
- Golda Klurman
- Masha Klurman
- Mordechai Drajcen
- Dvora'le Drajcen
- Moisha'le Drajcen

- Tzvi Klurman
- Lemma Klurman

Masha Drajcen — Yehezkiel Wolfsthal

Aba Klurman — Sisel Likvornik

- Dina Klurman
- Dvora Klurman
- Menucha Klurman
- Tzipora Klurman

Karin Alhassid — Yaron Wolfsthal

Limor Wolfsthal — Ron Yahal

- Yotam Wolfsthal
- Lior Wolfsthal
- Damian Kaliroff
- Yoad Wolfsthal
- Nimrod Yahal
- Yarden Yahal
- Shay Yahal

- Eitan

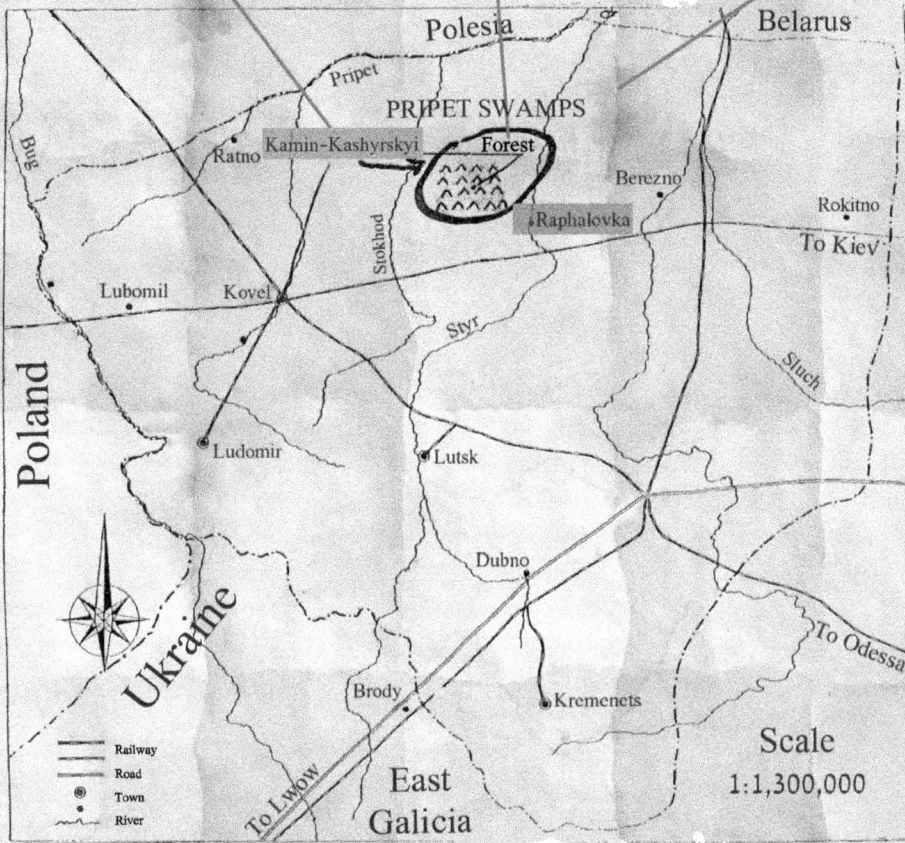

Polesia	Belarus

PRIPET SWAMPS

Pripet

Ratno • Kamin-Kashyrskyi   Forest

Berezno •

Rokitno •

Raphalovka

To Kiev

Bug

Stokhod

Lubomil •

Kovel •

Styr

Sluch

Poland

Ludomir •

Lutsk •

Ukraine

Dubno •

To Odessa

Brody •

Kremenets •

To Lwow

East
Galicia

Scale
1:1,300,000

— Railway
— Road
⊙ Town
⋯ River

My Roadmap

Kamin-Kashyrskyi

Kamin-Kashyrskyi is a town in north-central Volyn Oblast, Ukraine. Founded in the Middle Ages, the first record of a Jewish presence in the town dates back to 1569. By the end of the 19th century, Jews made up the majority of its population, at around 1,000 residents.

At the outbreak of World War I, the people of Kamin-Kashyrskyi were drafted into the Russian army. Upon its withdrawal in 1935, the town became filled with refugees, and the Cossack battalions that had been in the rear began committing acts of robbery, arson, and vandalism throughout the region. Eventually, the Austrian army came in and transferred control over the area to the army of the German Empire. The Russian-German front was halted near Kamin-Kashyrskyi, where it stayed until after the February Revolution of 1917 and the German takeover of Ukraine. Following the Riga Agreement in 1921, the town became part of Poland.

Between the two World Wars, at a time when control over the region was being passed around between the neighboring countries, about a third of Kamin-Kashyrskyi's population was Jewish – approximately 1,700 people. Most made a living from petty trade and various crafts, and were supported by community organizations and by the JDC[3]. Among the Jewish organizations operating in Kamin-Kashyrskyi were a union of Jewish merchants, a Hebrew school, a Jewish library, a community drama class, and for a time, a beit midrash[4]. Additionally, the area was rife with Zionist activity, with branches of almost all major Zionist youth movements. Kamin's youth was comprised almost entirely of Zionist young men and women who aspired to make Aliyah (immigrate to the Holy Land for reasons of Zionism). Some had even

---

[3] From Wikipedia: "The American Jewish Joint Distribution Committee, also known as the Joint or the JDC [...] is a global Jewish humanitarian aid and relief organization. [...] [Its purpose] is to offer aid to the many Jewish populations in central and eastern Europe, as well as in the Middle East, through a network of social initiatives and community assistance programs. In addition, the JDC donates millions of dollars for disaster relief causes and the development of non-Jewish communities".

[4] A Beit Midrash (also Beis Medrash or Beth Midrash; Hebrew: בֵּית מִדְרָשׁ, lit. "House of Learning", plural: Batei Midrash) is a Jewish study hall located in a synagogue, yeshiva, kollel, or other type of Jewish religion-oriented public space. It is distinct from a synagogue in that its primary purpose is studying Torah, as opposed to being a place of worship.

immigrated to the Land of Israel prior to the outbreak of World War II. At the time of the outbreak, the Jewish community in Kamin had more than 2,000 members.

In September 1939, the Russians conquered and occupied Poland as per the Ribbentrop-Molotov Pact between Germany and the Soviet Union. During this relatively quiet period, the town underwent a process of Sovietization in education, economics, and social life, and had seemingly been spared the horrors of the war. Schools were prohibited from teaching in Hebrew, and thus the Hebrew school started to teach in Yiddish instead. The curriculum was adjusted to fit Soviet values and beliefs, and all Zionist and Jewish activity in the region was discontinued.

In June 1941, the Germans moved to capture the Eastern Front as part of 'Operation Barbarossa'. Upon the Soviets' withdrawal from Poland, Kamin-Kashyrskyi was left without rule until July 16, when a German military government was established in the region. Ukrainian gangs and local peasants roamed the streets mugging, raping, and murdering the town's Jews.

On June 1, 1942, all Jewish residents in town, as well as Jews from the surrounding villages, were ordered to move into the densely overcrowded, newly established Kamin-Kashyrskyi ghetto, separated by a fence from the rest of the town. In the first Aktion on August 10, 1942, about 2,400 of the ghetto Jews were taken to killing pits and murdered on the spot. After the mass murder, about 600 young people with a "skilled worker's certificate" remained in the ghetto. Some escaped to the surrounding forests to find a weapon and join the Soviet partisans roaming the region.

On November 2, 1942, the ghetto was finally terminated in one final Aktion. Nearly 200 of its inhabitants were murdered, and about 400 managed to escape. In the winter of 1943, some of the escapees were murdered by partisan gangs, local farmers, or nationalist Ukrainians, and others succumbed to the cold and hunger. Only about 100 of them survived in partisan units, later joining the ranks of the Red Army. After the liberation by the Allies, the Jews who remained did not return to the town and became refugees. Some immigrated to Israel and some to other countries.

Out of approximately 3,000 Jews who lived in the Kamin-Kashyrskyi area in the beginning of 1942, only about 100 survived.

An Unforgettable Childhood in the Town of Kamin-Kashyrskyi

1

To think about my childhood is to conjure up little memories – or rather, short fragments – of vividly clear moments from a world long forgotten, most of which is still shrouded in mist. To think about my childhood is to randomly stumble upon it in unexpected moments, and watch as it resurfaces from deep within the forgotten recesses of my mind, to appear before me as if it had not been lost to time so many years ago.

A typical Jewish house

For example... On Hanukkah eve, the children and grandchildren come to visit us at our Haifa home. Yehezkel lights the traditional Hanukkah Menorah as the room fills with the sweet, appetizing aroma of the traditional Hanukkah latkes & jelly doughnuts I made, and our small apartment is completely engulfed in holiday spirit and heartwarming family hubbub. And suddenly I think I hear the doorbell ringing... Or maybe it's the door to my memory... and I see my paternal grandparents walking down the lane connecting our town to their village... And right then and there, the door opens wide and they enter, bringing with them a joyful aura and giving me Hanukkah gelt.[5]

And right after that, another picture pops into my mind, of their home in that remote green village, with the cattle grazing in their yard... Followed by a flashback to Grandpa's old gristmill, and the great fire which broke out one day and quickly demolished the gristmill along with the house, until nothing was left... Nothing but sorrow.

---

[5] The Yiddish term "Hanukkah gelt" (Yiddish: חנוכה געלט, Hebrew: דְּמֵי חֲנוּכָּה dmei ḥanukah, lit. "Hanukkah money") refers to pocket money traditionally given out by adults to children as a Hanukkah gift.

And then I see Mother, rushing after me to school because I had forgotten to take the breakfast she'd made for me… She enters the classroom and hands me the paper-wrapped sandwich, and I feel a little embarrassed in front of the other kids, not comfortable with everyone seeing Mother run after me to school.

Another sweet memory lets me once again experience the wonderful taste of Grandma's special chocolate confections; especially the candy she so enthusiastically made on that happy day when the last granddaughter of the family was born. And in my ears, I can still hear the melody of her words, passionately explaining to me that a postpartum mother must eat sweet things!

And then comes another lovely picture, that looks like it was taken right out of a princess fairytale… I am about four years old, it's a cold winter morning and Mother has dressed me up in a beautiful blue coat adorned by white velvet. A carriage is parked outside, and the three of us – Father, Mother and I – head out to roam the many forest roads and lanes surrounding town. And the reason for all of this is that I have fallen ill with the whooping cough, and the doctor has recommended that the child's lungs be treated with a dose of fresh air and magical green. And in this moment, there isn't a single soul happier or more important than me in the entire world.

I was born on the 3rd of March in the year 1932, the eldest daughter of my mother Freidel Plot and my father Zelig Drajcen, in a town by the name of Kamin-Kashyrskyi in eastern Poland. I was given the name Masha after my maternal grandfather, Moshe Plot.

We were four siblings: my brother Moisha'le (Moshe, the Hebrew name for Moses) who was four years younger than me, my sister Dvora'le (Deborah) who was about seven years younger than me – about whom everyone always said she was beautiful and sweet as a doll – and my baby brother Mordechai Lipa'le, who was just eighteen months old when I saw him for the last time.

At the age of six, I started going to the local Hebrew school by the name of HaTchiya (meaning "The Revival"), where all the teachers were Jewish, the

Freidel and Zelig Drajcen

curriculum was Zionism-oriented, and the official language was Hebrew! I was an honors student and received much praise. I loved studying and dedicated myself to schoolwork with utmost devotion.

I remember my first teacher, young and pretty Bat-Sheva, who taught me in the first and second grades and of whom I was very fond. At the end of the school year, she joined an Aliyah training program in Poland, traveled to the Land of Israel and disappeared from our lives forever. Before she left, all the kids in class went over to her house and brought her a photo album to remember us by in the faraway Land of Israel.

Not every household in Poland was Zionist, but in my family, the ideas of Zionism and dreams about the Land of Israel ran side by side with the traditional Jewish lifestyle. While we spoke Yiddish at home, we also owned books in Hebrew, and I was even subscribed to a Hebrew children's newspaper called "Olami HaKatan" (meaning "My Little World"), whose cover featured the likeness of renowned Jewish poet Hayim Nachman Bialik, who in time would become known as Israel's national poet.

Father also participated in a Zionist convention in Warsaw at one time, and the idea of the Land of Israel – specifically the concept of making Aliyah – was a very prevalent topic of discussion around the house.

In fact, our entire town was very Jewish and very Zionist. Synagogues and Batei Midrash existed alongside branches of several Zionist political movements, namely Beitar (an acronym for "Brit Yosef Trumpeldor", meaning "The Joseph Trumpeldor Alliance"), HaShomer HaTzair (meaning "The Young Guard"), and HaPoel HaMizrachi (meaning "The Mizrachi[6] Worker"). Just near our home, down the street, stood two Batei Midrash, one named "Triskr Shchol" and another named "Stepanir Shtibl". Father would mostly attend the former, though other members of the family preferred the latter.

On Sabbath evenings, I remember my mother and grandmother lighting Sabbath candles at home. Grandma would bless the candles with her crystal candlesticks and Mother would do the same with glass ones. After that, as a Mitzvah, they would put some coins into two charity boxes: the first was a Rabbi Meir Ba'al HaNes one, and the second was a Jewish National Fund donation box called a Blue Box, for redemption of lands in Israel.

Each year in the days leading up to Passover, the house would be thoroughly cleaned in preparation for the holiday. Grandma and Mother would open the double-glass windows to bring in fresh air from outside and bring our beautiful Passover-only kitchenware out of storage, among which was even a special Passover-only ashtray that had not come in contact with any chametz[7]. Every Passover, each one of us would also be given two custom-tailored suits that Mother would order from Nekhamka, our seamstress neighbor – one for holidays and Sabbath, and one for regular weekdays. I remember the last one that was sewed for me: it was a Bordeaux-colored dress, made out of a soft, fluffy material pleasant to the touch, with two sewn-on buttons adorning it from the front.

---

[6] From Wikipedia: Mizrahi Jews (Hebrew: יְהוּדֵי הַמִּזְרָח‎), Mizrahim (מִזְרָחִים) [...] ,or Oriental Jews are the descendants of Jews from local Jewish communities in the Middle East and North Africa."

[7] The term chametz (Hebrew: חָמֵץ‎, lit. "leaven") refers to foods with leavening agents, forbidden by the Jewish law during the days of Passover.

Every Saturday, Grandma would take the book of prayers in her hand and head to the synagogue to pray in the women's section. Mother only joined her on holidays, and I only joined them on Rosh Hashanah, when all the families in town got together in the synagogue and the feeling of holiday festivity rested upon all. Among my memories from the synagogue is the face of Sonia, a girl my age whom we affectionately called Slonechka, like the Polish word for "sun". Sonia had been orphaned from her father and I pitied her. I remember everyone praying Yizkor in the synagogue on Yom Kippur and then proceeding out into the streets, while only Sonia stayed inside just a little longer, longing for her father.

The town rabbi was a man by the name of Rabbi Perlin, whom everyone held in very high regard. To this day I can still vividly see him in my mind's eye, with his ever-presentable appearance and his kind, beard-covered face. I remember the face of his very pretty daughter as well. They lived right next to our school, and every morning I would pass by their house on my way there. It was important to me to be the first one in class, and I would walk quickly – or rather, run – fighting against the freezing cold, constantly calculating how much further I still had to go, as their house and our school were separated only by a narrow road I had to cross.

I felt very loved and protected in childhood. My family was always proud and satisfied with me, showering me with attention and giving me nicknames such as "Dreidel", meaning spinning top, and "kweksilber", meaning quicksilver. People would always say about me that I "had to be in the know about everything, be included in everything, see everything, be everywhere". I would bombard Father with all kinds of different questions, and he would always gladly and willingly take a break from his busy schedule to explain things to me and expose me to new horizons.

My mother Freidel was born to my grandmother in a triplet birth but was the only one of the three to survive childbirth. My grandmother affectionately called her "Miss Straw Woman" because of how frail and delicate she had been in childhood. Even after she married my father, Grandma never stopped caring for her, even moving in with us to help around the house.

I loved Grandma more than anything in the world. She would cook all my favorite foods just for me, among which was a wonderful millet porridge. I used to sometimes peel the paint off the house walls, and my mother would get angry with me, trying to no avail to wean me off this bad habit. Grandma would always say to her, "leave the child be… She could be low on calcium".

Feeling as loved and wanted as I did, I would sometimes turn out to be extremely stubborn, not budging an inch from my position until my wishes were fulfilled. I remember one time when I was fiercely angry about something, I declared a "broyges"[8] on my parents and refused to take it back. Father demanded I apologize, but I absolutely refused. I was fortified in my anger and left the house in protest. The weather was unbearably cold that day, and no one except me dared to even think about staying outside. I hid under the drainpipes that came down from the roof, all the while wishing and praying that the rain would drip right into my ears and cause me to catch a severe cold, and it would be my parents' fault that I got sick, and they would be very sorry and ask me for forgiveness. I don't know how long I waited there until my parents finally caved in and rushed to get me inside. My father was truly angry with me, even threatening to hit me so that I'd finally learn a lesson. I remember telling him that even if he hurt me, I wouldn't learn. I held fiercely to my will to win! Eventually, he changed his mind and ended up giving me no punishment at all. In the end I really did get sick, and everyone felt sorry and was very concerned for me.

When my brother Moisha'le was born, I was standing outside the house playing ball. I was about five years old at the time and had been sent outside so as not to disturb the others. I remember standing outside the window, yelling: "Mother, is it a boy or a girl?" I don't remember her response, but I do know she gave birth indoors, with the help of Grandma and a midwife.

All the other houses around us belonged to Jews as well, and I only got to see our gentile neighbors when visiting Father at the store. Father made a living selling iron – mainly plows and other kinds of farming equipment.

---

[8] A Yiddish term meaning "angry", "in a fight" or "not on speaking terms".

Our store was successful and had a very central place in town. A large portion of our customers were gentiles from the surrounding villages who made a living from farming and working off the land. Mother helped out at the store and left the responsibility of household duties in the capable hands of Grandma.

I remember Mother liked to dress up. She had a box of face powder, makeup, and skin creams, as well as a checkered raincoat she would sometimes wear on her trips to the big city of Kovel. She also had a number of elegant dresses, ordered from the town seamstress specifically to serve as Sabbath-only attire, and the hats to match.

Every Saturday, a gentile lady by the name of Flashka or Mlashka would come to our house to work as a "Shabbos (Sabbath) goy[9]": Since she was not Jewish, she could perform any task which the Jewish law of the Sabbath prevented us from doing ourselves, such as turning on the oven to heat up food.

In the living room, next to a large brick wall, stood a hearth which was itself made of bricks. The bricks in the wall absorbed the heat of the hearth and filled our home with pleasant warmth. On cold winter Saturdays, we would enjoy sitting on the bench by the wall and feeling nice and cozy. The same bench was also used to warm up all our bedding, pillows, and blankets before we got into bed.

Another Saturday pleasure was having Grandma's cookies delivered right up to my bed in the morning. They were incredibly delicious confections made of butter and chocolate. All week long I would look forward to this ritual, which would be carried out for months every year, up until right after the holiday of Purim, when Mother and Grandma would begin to gradually prepare the house for Passover. They had to make sure there wasn't any residue of chametz left anywhere in the house, which also meant no flour, and no more delicious cookies.

---

[8] In modern Hebrew and Yiddish, the word "goy" (Hebrew: גּוֹי, plural: "גּוֹיִים", transliterated "goyim", or "goys") refers to a gentile – a non-Jewish person. The female variant is "goya" (Hebrew: גּוֹיָה).

Those were good years. A young family, an eldest daughter and her younger siblings, with many relatives – uncles, aunts, and cousins – living either in the same town or in the nearby area. So much future was ahead of us all. So many get-togethers, joys and hopes. And the memories… The memories of those days are embedded in me, and when they come to life, I watch them as if I'm flipping through the pages of a precious photo album, and become full of longing.

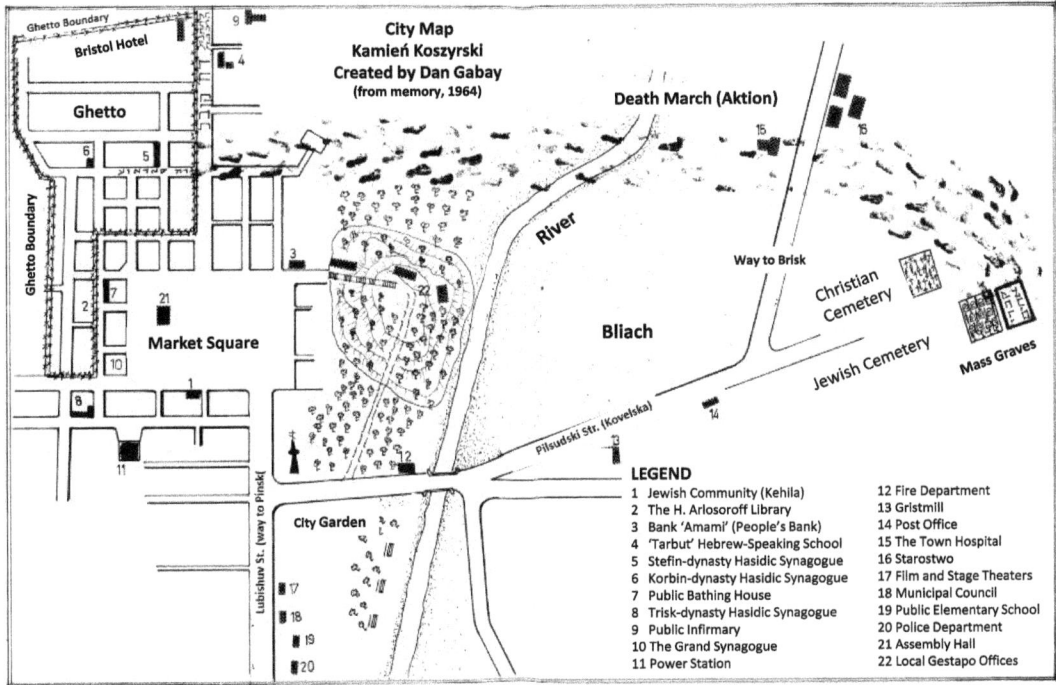

City Map
Kamień Koszyrski
Created by Dan Gabay
(from memory, 1964)

Ghetto Boundary

Bristol Hotel

Ghetto

Ghetto Boundary

Death March (Aktion)

River

Way to Brisk

Christian Cemetery

Bliach

Jewish Cemetery

Mass Graves

Market Square

Pilsudski Str. (Kovelska)

Lubishuv St. (way to Pinsk)

City Garden

LEGEND

1 Jewish Community (Kehila)
2 The H. Arlosoroff Library
3 Bank 'Amami' (People's Bank)
4 'Tarbut' Hebrew-Speaking School
5 Stefin-dynasty Hasidic Synagogue
6 Korbin-dynasty Hasidic Synagogue
7 Public Bathing House
8 Trisk-dynasty Hasidic Synagogue
9 Public Infirmary
10 The Grand Synagogue
11 Power Station

12 Fire Department
13 Gristmill
14 Post Office
15 The Town Hospital
16 Starostwo
17 Film and Stage Theaters
18 Municipal Council
19 Public Elementary School
20 Police Department
21 Assembly Hall
22 Local Gestapo Offices

The Market Square, 1930

Kovel Street

27

The Russians Arrive,
a Change of Regime

2

In September 1939, following the outbreak of World War II, the Russians invaded Poland as part of The Molotov–Ribbentrop Pact signed between Germany and The Soviet Union, and subsequently entered our town. Within mere days, we effectively became part of the latter, and our lives changed beyond recognition. On the one hand, we did enjoy some level of comfort: Poland was spared a German occupation and we became equal citizens in every way. Jews and Ukrainians could now be accepted into jobs and roles that had previously been off-limits for them. But on the other hand, all Polish and Jewish community institutions were closed down, including the Hebrew school I had been attending, and Zionist activity was declared illegal. Schools were now prohibited from teaching in Hebrew, so we began studying in Yiddish and Russian instead. In addition, a government warrant compelled both schools and businesses to open on Saturday, which contrasted with the Jewish law of the Sabbath. Being in school also meant we had to engage in writing on Saturday, which in itself was forbidden. These laws were perceived as a terrible decree impossible to follow. It was a huge burden on everyone, and was the source for a great deal of agony. In the months that followed, Jewish stores were nationalized altogether and became property of the state. This included Father's store.

Jews who leaned towards a socialist ideology were happy with the change and welcomed the Russians' arrival in Poland. We, however, were not happy with the new regime, and struggled to adapt to the new way of life. My parents were in a constant state of unease.

Rumors had it that people of the upper-middle class, referred to by the Russians as "bourgeoisie", were being forcefully sent to Siberia. Public religious activity had shrunk down considerably, and any discussion about the Land of Israel now had to be in secret. Daily life became much harder under the constant fear of the authorities.

My father in the Polish army artillery corps uniform

That period turned out to be quite short, however, lasting only about eighteen months. I remember it primarily for being the time when Russian and Ukrainian became the official languages of Poland, and all schools – including mine – were required to teach in Ukrainian instead of Hebrew. Being the young and curious child I was, I easily picked up the new language, and within mere weeks became a proudly fluent Ukrainian speaker. My teacher Shlomo Zaltz was impressed by my clear handwriting and fast speech, and asked me to copy articles from the school newspaper onto the school bulletin board.

During the last few months of the Soviet regime, many Jews in town – including my father – were drafted into the Red Army and had to say goodbye to their families for an unknown period of time. Years prior, Father had served as an artillery soldier in the Polish Army, and my parents had a lovely large picture of him in military uniform on their bedroom wall. Years later, after I had settled in Israel, someone sent me a smaller version of that same picture, but alas, I have lost it.

Father was drafted into the cavalry. He was tasked with taking care of four horses and making sure they were in fit condition. In the first few weeks following his draft, I would go with Mother to visit him at a military camp not far from us, in a small forest on the outskirts of town. He would treat us to delicious waffles he'd buy at the base canteen, and I would always come out of those visits feeling happy and content.

Mother, however, always cried when it was time to go. She feared what was to come. She didn't know when she and Father would get to see each other again, and whether his unit would remain stationed nearby or move someplace else. She was worried about what was going to happen to us all. The tension could be felt everywhere, and rumors kept spreading about a coming danger. Eventually, Father surprised us when he unexpectedly returned home after a few weeks. I can still vividly remember the house door opening wide to reveal him standing there in military uniform. He told us there had been a bombing and an overwhelming number of blasts suddenly started raining down on camp. The horses panicked, broke through the fences, and ran away in all directions. Some of the soldiers who served alongside him ran east after the Russian army into the depths of Russia, to homefront territory.

But amidst the tension in the air, Father decided to come home and be with us. I know today that those who ran into Russia were able to reach the Ural Mountains, and most of them survived the war. We got to see Father again and welcome him home, and it is thanks to him that I am alive today.

The joy and relief we felt from seeing him filled us with strength. No longer were we just a mother, a grandmother and three little children. When Father returned, a sense of security returned to our lives with him, and we were once again a whole family. Though he was tired, worn-out, and concerned about what the future may hold, his return to us and Mother's sigh of relief abolished any feelings of fear of the impending war from our hearts.

The German Occupation, Summer 1942

3

Unfortunately, that brief period of relief went by so quickly, and was so overshadowed by the turmoil and gloom that followed, that our few happy days together were all but wiped from my memory, never to be found again.

That terrible day when the Germans invaded Kamin… I remember it like it was just a moment ago, like I'm still standing there… a little girl about nine years-old, standing there and watching everything as it happens...

In June of 1942, the Germans stormed into Poland. I seem to remember they came riding on motorcycles, and everyone panicked and rushed into their homes to hide from them. It was clear to me that something terrible was happening. Father forbade me from going outside to walk among the people. A strange and unfamiliar feeling spread through the streets, and even though I didn't entirely understand what was going on, I knew that our lives were all in great danger. The Russians, who up until the day before had been a part of our lives and of daily affairs in town, disappeared without a trace.

Father didn't believe the Germans.

He knew with absolute certainty that they could not be trusted. I don't know what the source of this confidence was – perhaps he knew this based on his short time in the Russian army, perhaps from meeting refugees who had escaped Poland, or perhaps from rumors among the adults – but from the moment the German occupation began, all of his thoughts, attention, and energy were focused solely on one thing: how to survive, how to save his family, and how to prepare for what's to come. It was as if he could already see a plain-as-day picture of the future that would befall us all.

The German occupation made us all immensely fearful. A thick, dark cloud of pure terror came down on the public overnight. It felt as though the light of the sun and the peaceful world we knew had been blocked by a veil of darkness and replaced by a new reality, dominated by colors of absolute gloom. Everyone kept saying the Germans were planning to kill us all, that it was going to happen very soon, that it was happening in other places as well. And Father, more than anyone, believed – or rather, knew – that there was truth to this chatter.

One morning, a group of German soldiers forcibly opened our house door and barged right in. They grabbed Mother and Grandma, aggressively dragged them outside, and loudly ordered them to stand by the wall. They both froze in terror. I couldn't help but burst into tears. From everything I'd heard the adults say, I knew that standing by the wall meant you were about to be shot dead. Grandma saw my crying and started begging the Germans… "Look… The little children are crying inside… Please have mercy on us, don't hurt us, don't kill us…"

I can't recall exactly what happened next – perhaps the German soldier never meant to shoot to begin with – but he let out a loud shout… "head back!" and in one moment, our tight bodies loosened and we were instantly rejuvenated and returned to life. I can't remember if Father was with us then, or if he was even home at the time, but I'll never forget the sight of Mother and Grandma leaning against the wall with the German soldiers holding their rifles. I'll never forget Mother's terrified, pale face, the voice of Grandma begging for mercy, or how my entire body was trembling as I stood there gasping for air, with everything hinging on the word of a single German soldier.

A few days later, the Germans rounded up a large group of men from all over town – among whom was Father – and locked them up inside a local church. We were all once again consumed by that same choking feeling of helplessness and didn't know what to do. The solution, that time, was bribing both the Germans and the Ukrainians. People went door to door all over town, collecting money from each and every family to pay the bail and release the people who had been locked up. It took a few days, and there was a heavy feeling in the air. No one knew for certain how much money would satisfy the Ukrainians, what plans and schemes they were brewing up, or exactly how we were supposed to get them to release the people they'd locked up. The suspense was palpable, and a sense of panic flooded the entire town and threatened to drown us all. We kept waiting for Father, praying for his safe return. And that was just the beginning.

In the face of this increasingly unstable new reality, a Jewish committee was formed: the Judenrat, as we called it. It was meant to act as a mediator between the public and the local German authorities. Each day the Germans surprised us with new orders passed down through the Judenrat. Every once in a while, a group of townsmen would allegedly be sent to work out of town, and would never be seen again. The Germans would put the men up on designated trucks, and none ever came back. Initially they only took young men capable of physical labor, but when no one returned, everyone knew they were never really sent to work anywhere, but were in fact no longer alive. From the shuttered homes to the whispery conversations among the people, a feeling of great distress was building up inside us all. The hearts of everyone were consumed with fear of the looming danger.

The entire Volyn Oblast was populated by many other Jewish communities much like our own, which all shared the same fate. From the moment the German occupation began, all communication between the towns was completely cut off. All roads were blocked, and Jews were prohibited from traveling on them. We essentially became isolated and hidden away from the outside world, trapped within the confines of town. Not long after that, we became even more restricted, completely confined to only the walls of the ghetto. Yet, despite having no communication with the outside world, we knew that this wasn't happening only in our town, but everywhere else as well. We knew that the Germans killed. Even I, a ten-year-old child, knew that much.

This is how things were back then – we lived with the knowledge that people wanted us dead.

One night, a rumor spread that something bad was going to happen. I was so afraid I couldn't sleep and remained awake for hours. Towards morning, as the shadows of night began to lift, I looked out the window and saw armed soldiers storming our neighbors' homes, grabbing terrified young men and forcefully dragging them out to the street. They were accompanied by a very large dog, so petrifying that the mere sight of it was enough to make one freeze in place. I heard shots and saw people falling to the ground. This went on and on, continuing well into the morning. The sunlight eventually revealed the houses, which up until then had been covered in darkness. By then, I could very clearly see what was happening. The shots exploded right in my ears. I swiftly opened the house door and made a run for the nearby synagogue where everyone was being rounded up. Someone had apparently tried to resist, or perhaps escape, and I saw him being shot right then and there, on the spot, before collapsing and falling to the pavement. I heard his words, too: "It's such a nice day and I'm going to die."

That was the first time I witnessed shooting; my first time seeing someone fall. Seeing what it actually meant to kill.

4 *Our Home in the Ghetto*

At the end of 1942, six months after the occupation began, we were ordered to evacuate our homes at once and move into the ghetto. The ghetto was bounded by a large fence, made of many wooden planks with a barb wire on top. The fence made it impossible to see the outside world. Every single building on the street – from residential homes to warehouses and storage facilities – was now being used to house families of Jews. More and more Jewish families were constantly being brought in from the surrounding villages, and the place became terribly overcrowded. At its peak, the number of Jews in the ghetto was as high as three thousand souls. Venturing outside the ghetto walls was strictly forbidden, and the only gate in the fence was guarded by Ukrainian officers at all times.

Fortunately for us, our house was already located within the borders of the newly established ghetto, so at least we didn't have to move out and leave all our property behind. We weren't short on food either, which was not to be taken for granted, since the ghetto was full of hungry people everywhere, with many households left with nothing to eat at all. I don't know exactly how things worked in the ghetto in terms of obtaining food and supporting oneself. I'm not sure whether the Germans brought food into the ghetto or if they just left us to our fate. Father showed great resourcefulness as always: thanks to the good relationships he had always maintained with the locals in the days before the occupation, he still managed to make trade with them, obtaining necessities such as flour, oil, potatoes, and sugar to store in our pantry. Despite the ever-growing hunger around the ghetto, our house always had enough food for all of us. Money was meaningless and of no value in the shut-off world of the ghetto, however, and any transaction was made through bartering what little remnants of property we still had left, such as golden coins we still had from the good old days.

Grandma and Mother would cook impromptu meals in the kitchen. They would keep the skins from any peeled potatoes and leave them to dry under the sun. Grandma explained to me that she was saving the skins for rough days when we would have no food left, and that when that time came, she would use them to make delicious latkes.

The general kitchen of the ghetto was not far from our home, and destitute residents on the verge of starvation would line up there every day. It was a sort of soup kitchen, apparently set up and run by the Judenrat. In the beginning, when it was still possible to come and go from the ghetto, gentile locals would come to sell their produce and trade goods with the Jews inside, some of whom still had different kinds of canned food in storage from the days of before the war.

All in all, we did our best to keep our old lifestyle in the face of the all-encompassing restrictions. The lady who had been working for our family for years as a "Shabbos goy" continued to come even after the ghetto was established, and I remember her sometimes arriving the day after Sabbath to receive her payment, since the Jewish law forbade Jews from making any kind of transaction on Sabbath.

Since school had been closed down, my parents, who had much faith and hope for the future, hired a tutor for me and my brother Moisha'le, who gave us lessons in a variety of school subjects as well as the Hebrew Bible.

5 *Setting Up Hiding Places*

The ghetto was eventually cut off from the outside world entirely, and people were no longer allowed to freely come and go. It was at that point that Father concluded we needed to make sure we would have a place to hide when worst came to worst. Being the ever-curious child I was, who just had to be in the know about everything, I stuck to him like glue and followed his every step around the house, not taking my eyes off him for a single moment. He tried to keep me away, to prevent me from seeing and understanding what he was doing, but I insisted. He began building a number of hideouts around the house. I remember three small ones and one large enough to fit the entire family. The small hideouts were built under our normal ceiling in the attic, pantry, and storeroom, and can best be described as double ceilings of sorts, each about half a meter high. Father also gave us exact instructions on how to act if the Germans ever broke into the house. He said I would have to go upstairs to the attic hideout and not rush out under any circumstances. I remember he took me up there several times and we went over and simulated what I'd have to do in the moment of truth. This was where I'd have to hide.

Danger was present in every step and stride along the way, and any distinction between the children's world and the adult one became a thing of the past. People came in and out, bringing with them stories they'd heard, rumors they'd picked up on, and every tidbit of information they'd managed to obtain. Everyone knew something, and information spread by word-of-mouth and reached all parts of the ghetto: from the streets, to the homes, to the tight and dank rooms therein.

At a later point in time, after the ghetto had been completely isolated, Father began building a large hideout inside the house. He installed another wall parallel to the house, that reached all the way up to the ceiling, creating a space approximately a-meter-and-a-half wide which could only be entered by crawling in from the pantry. The pantry itself was dark and obscured. Father had piled up many logs of wood around the entrance, and it blended perfectly with the environment. No one would ever have guessed that there were people hiding behind that wall. Work on constructing the hideout was only done at night while everyone was fast asleep, so as not to draw attention to ourselves, especially from potential snitches. I was present throughout the entire process, and little by little, Father was making me into his little partner; he wanted to make sure that when the time came, I would act exactly as instructed.

And me – I remained in a constant state of high alert, doing my best not to miss out on any piece of information, trying my hardest to read the adults' facial expressions, to follow Father's every instruction, and most importantly: not to fall into their hands; not to let the Germans kill us.

In the entire time we were in the ghetto, not once did Father leave the confines of its walls. He was never sent by the Germans on any labor jobs, either. He must have managed to avoid showing up whenever they issued a work warrant. He held neither a work permit nor a permit to leave the ghetto. He chose not to trust the Germans, and reiterated to us again and again that we must never believe their word. Whenever they sent out an order for everyone to gather somewhere, such as when we had to go through routine checkups, we would promptly enter one of our hideouts and wait for whatever was happening outside to pass.

Our family had a Christian friend who lived in the nearby village of Verkhy. Father believed with all his heart that she was his true friend and trusted her completely. One day, at the time when it was still possible to freely come and go from the ghetto, he invited her over and they sat down for a conversation of a few hours. I knew Father was planning to hand over a considerable portion of our family property to her for safekeeping. He apparently signed an agreement with her that if, God forbid, the unthinkable happens and he can no longer protect me, she will take me in to raise as one of her own and keep me safe from harm. The residents of Verkhy had known Father since the day he was born. My grandparents still lived there, too, as they would not leave the place until later when the ghetto was terminated along with the rest of the Jews in the region. She was the owner of a successful sawmill, and Father held her in very high regard, both for her skill and for her good nature. This meeting took place in 1942, mere months after the occupation began, at a time when there was still hope that rays of light would shine through the darkness that had befallen us.

After she went on her way, Father asked me what I thought about the option of going to live with her. After all, he said, she had no children of her own, and my presence would surely make her very happy. He added that the situation in the ghetto was very dire and we had to act wisely and prepare for what's to come. Father treated me like a mature adult in a conversation between two people examining the situation together, trying to decide on the most appropriate solution given the circumstances. He took the time to explain to me why it would be for the best, why it was necessary, why it would be the wisest choice. His words of persuasion, though patent and warm, were very painful to hear, and fell on deaf ears. I remained steadfast in my refusal and simply refused to listen. My answer was a resounding "no." "I'm not going anywhere," I said. "I'm not leaving you, or Mother, or Grandma, or my little brothers. I'm staying home and not going to that woman." I was relieved when Father didn't bring up her name again afterwards, and that conversation, like many others, left my mind. I thought I must have swayed him from the idea. The woman visited us a couple more times after that, each time receiving money from him.

6 The Final Aktion and the Hideout in the Attic

On August 2, 1942, a hot summer day, the biggest Aktion yet took place in the ghetto.

The German word "Aktion" (meaning "action") was the term used by the Germans to describe the act of terminating a ghetto along with all of the Jews therein. In the time leading up to the final Aktion, we could feel it coming. A wave of rumors had been flooding the streets, claiming something truly horrific was going to happen. One could not hope to avoid these murmurs, or the sense of dread they brought with them. There was no escaping the overwhelming panic that took hold of everyone and the feeling of terror clutching at the throat.

We woke up in the morning to the sounds of shouting, yelling and ear-piercing screams. There was a horrible ruckus outside. We were told everyone had to come out of their homes because the Germans and their Ukrainian collaborators were conducting a search, looking through each and every house for secret stashes of weapons. Father immediately pieced together what was happening. No one leaves the house, he said, and instructed us all to hurry and hide – some in the large hideout and the rest in the smaller hiding spots around the house. As in previous times, we snuck into the hiding spots in spite of the Germans' orders, in spite of the sounds of booming gunshots, and in spite of the fear that came over us, and waited inside, completely still and utterly silent, praying that we survive and make it through it all.

A few months beforehand, I began to hear chatter about the partisans among the adults. I remember that the word itself was new to me and was mostly uttered in whisper. They kept saying that it was vital for us to acquire weapons for self-defense, but also that our inability to leave the ghetto made that impossible, let alone the fact that there was no one to buy from. Father started talking about escaping the ghetto, saying we needed to head out into the woods. It was clear to him that staying in the ghetto was a death sentence, and that we were running out of time. He knew death was on every door, and that if we wanted to live, we had to find a way to escape. But how? We were four small children, a feeble mother and an elderly grandmother. How would we all be able to escape the ghetto, which would require walking out a gate guarded by armed Ukrainian officers with hatred coursing through their veins and murder in their eyes? The situation was desperately impossible.

When the Aktion started, we quickly rushed into the hideout behind the wall, which was completely concealed by a pile of wooden logs and could only be accessed by crawling Inside. Father had installed a large barrel in the hideout, filled with water which would last us a few days. Mother and Grandma had cooked and prepared everything required to sustain us, taking care to specifically make deliciously sweet jello which was my little brothers' favorite food. They also made sure to pack warm blankets and appropriate clothing for all of us, doing their best to make sure the hours ahead would be as comfortable as possible.

The operation was meticulously planned and it seemed like everything had been taken into consideration, down to the smallest detail. We could hear the Germans beyond the wall, constantly yelling and ordering people to come out. They were very intimidating, swearing and cursing as they slammed doors with the butts of their rifles. I put my hands on my ears trying to shut out all the noise. Like all the other times prior, Father instructed us to enter the hideout and not come out until the Aktion was over, no matter what. Other members of the family rushed into the hideout as well and stayed there in complete silence, anxiously awaiting whatever was to come next.

Grandma Feige-Rosi, whom I loved more than anything in the world and who loved me immensely as well, approached Father and said: "I'm an old woman, not young like the rest of you. Our worst fears are coming true. I'm not going into the hideout with you; I'll go with little Lipa'le and Dvora'le into the small hideout upstairs. I'll bring the jello with me to help calm them if the need arises." Father obliged and helped her climb up the ladder to the hideout in the attic, bringing my two brothers on up after her. "If, God forbid, the Germans get here, and if, God forbid, the children start crying and even the jello doesn't calm them down and they give us away… I'd like to hope the rest of you will survive in the larger hideout." She likely believed she'd be able to calm the little ones and that we would all be spared the tragedy.

She got no argument from Father. All in all, we were about thirty relatives hiding together in the large hideout, most of whom were from my mother and grandmother's side. My grandmother took my three-year-old sister Dvora'le and my eighteen-months-old brother Mordechai Lipa and climbed up to the impromptu hideout Father had built under the ceiling. He shut the doors, covered the entrances, and instructed us all to keep completely silent.

We went through the first few days feeling completely cut off from everything. We had no way of knowing what was happening outside. Freezing in the hideout, we kept hearing all sorts of sounds and noises from the outside world and didn't know what to make of them. Suddenly, in one moment, the silence was abruptly broken. We could clearly hear the voices of Germans loudly and forcibly pushing the entrance door and breaking into the house. They went from room to room, tapping on the walls to find possible spaces while spouting out things in German. It didn't take long for them to find the small hideout where Grandma was staying along with my little brothers. Maybe one of them made a sound. Maybe my baby brother Lipa'le started crying. They yelled and shouted as they forced them down the stairs and stormed out of the house, leaving us all in utter shock.

I remember we all continued to keep silent. We didn't move. Didn't exchange a word. We barely even breathed. My whole body was hurting from the struggle not to cry. I was frozen solid and didn't move a muscle, not looking in my parents' eyes. Everyone else was the same: holding their breath, looking like they were already dead. And Mother… My young, beautiful Mother… I saw the light in her eyes go out right in front of me. Her very liveliness drained away from her face and was lost forever.

She took my brother and me in for a hug with her tired hands, and as she did, I knew that my mother, the person I knew and loved, was gone forever. It all happened in seconds. We didn't hear Grandma going down the ladder. All we heard was Dvora'le's and Lipa'le's crying. We never let out as much as a sound. We each retreated into ourselves, petrified and stricken with shock. I hugged

Mother tightly. I clung close to her, brought my head in under her embrace and stroked her. I wanted so much to help her in her pain. Even though I didn't understand what exactly was happening or what was going to happen, somewhere deep inside I understood what it meant to be a mother, what it felt like to have maternal instincts, and the unimaginable pain she was feeling in those moments.

7 *After the Aktion*

The rest of the day went by in tense silence. Suddenly, we began to hear loud knocking noises. We didn't know what to make of them. It was our third day in the hideout. The clear sounds of knocking continued on-and-off for the next few hours, and only stopped around nighttime. We tried speculating as to what exactly was happening outside, but we couldn't know for certain. When the darkness of night descended, we suddenly heard Jews calling out in Yiddish: "Yidelekh… Yidelekh (Jews… Jews…") … It's over now… Anyone still alive can come… It's done… The slaughter is over..."

The voices we heard were crying out in agony. Even so, we dared not trust their words, and weren't sure how to act. When the sky was completely dark, Father decided to carefully come out of the hideout along with my uncle Shevach Bergman, who was also in the hideout with us, and check what the situation was outside. They quietly crawled out of the hideout, upon which they discovered the reason for all the noise and continuous knocking: the Germans had completely changed the face of the ghetto with the Aktion, narrowing its borders and installing a new fence that sealed off what little terrain had been left after most of its residents had been ruthlessly murdered. We soon found out that our home was now outside the borders of the ghetto – in fact, it was right on the border.

Father was forced to find a new hiding place for us within the ghetto's narrow new borders. We moved into an empty apartment where Moisha'le and I spent most of our days cooped up in the basement. From then on, we stopped coming out to the outside world altogether.

About twenty-five-hundred people were brutally murdered in this Aktion, thrown into killing pits dug in advance by Ukrainian collaborators.

We later learned how a large portion of the town's Jews had been forcefully led to the Kamin cemetery, located about two or three kilometers away from where we lived. The Germans had called out the names of the people and

45

murdered them in a predetermined order. The children and the elderly were first in line. The Germans forcefully separated the children from their parents and murdered them one after another.

My aunt didn't want to go on living after her children were murdered, and went into the killing pit after them despite the fact she could have stayed alive that day, as she had recently been granted a work permit and could have returned to the ghetto after the Aktion.

The cemetery was tight and terribly overcrowded. People were shouting and yelling in fear, and a terrible sense of chaos consumed all.

The massacre went on for three days. Jews from the surrounding villages were also brought in and murdered in the same fashion. Among them were my grandmother and grandfather and their entire family, including Father's brothers and sisters.

While we could hear the echoes of gunshots in the deep silence of the hideout, we never imagined the scope of the atrocity. We couldn't have. We were focused on the brutal stress we ourselves were under, in our struggle not to give ourselves away with the faintest of noises, the tiniest of movements, or the smallest whiff of air.

By the end of the Aktion, no children were left in the ghetto. My brother and I were among the very few children still alive in Kamin-Kashyrskyi. Perhaps a small handful survived in other hideouts throughout town. The survivors wouldn't stop talking about the fact that the children had been murdered. Those who were spared the slaughter thanks to possessing work permits had all suffered a terrible trauma. They'd all lost their families. Their children.

The knowledge there were no more children around affected me greatly. Being just about the only child in the world, realizing all my friends were gone, knowing that a living, healthy girl was a rare sight these days… And Father even told us, "We can't let anyone see living children."

8 *Last Days in the Basement*

The basement Father found for us seemed like a safe place to stay. He forbade us from leaving its walls without permission. But by that point, I didn't need Father's orders to make me stay inside; I knew nothing good was going to happen any time soon. I feared the Germans, the Ukrainians, and what few people remained in the ghetto after the Aktion. For three whole months I stayed in there, not going outside once. For three whole months I didn't see a strip of sky, a stretch of street, a square of green. I spent the time surrounded by the silence of the basement, along with my mother and my little brother. On some days it would be just the three of us, cut off and far away from the rest of humanity. We no longer lived with our other relatives, and I had no knowledge of their fate, their whereabouts, or even if they were still alive. The vacant ghetto was full of dreary, empty apartments, and everyone found their own secluded spot to retreat to. All I could see was my parents' distress and the loneliness that had befallen us, which seemed to only be getting worse by the day.

The days went by with little to no speaking. We didn't study, we didn't play, we didn't do anything. The fear had shrunk our lives down into virtually nothing. The harsh living conditions badly affected the handful of Jews who were still in the ghetto. Snitches would occasionally sell out other Jews to the Germans, and it was important to exercise caution and put faith in no one. Whenever my parents left for work so they could get food for everyone, Father warned me not to make a sound and not to put my head or hands out of the basement. He was terrified of what would happen if anyone discovered us and snitched, if it became known that there were still living children in the ghetto – because if, God forbid, that happened, it would be the end of us all.

This solitude imposed upon us proved very difficult for me to bear. While I did have Father and Mother with me, and my brother Moisha'le, it wasn't the same anymore. Our liveliness was gone, as well as our initial hopes that the war was going to end soon. Mother's sorrow covered the basement with a thick blanket of sadness.

One morning, Father entered the basement and told Mother that he had a bad feeling that something terrible was going to happen once more. People had been saying there was going to be another Aktion. "We cannot wait. We must escape the ghetto now." It was Sunday, November 2, 1942, exactly three months after the previous Aktion.

Mother was very weak by that point, and her spirit completely broken. My brother Moisha'le was lying in bed in the corner of the room. He had fallen ill with dysentery and an ear infection, and was slowly fading right before our eyes. He very clearly needed to see a doctor. Mother looked at Father. "No… I don't want to escape," she uttered quietly. "I have no more strength left. You take Mashinka and escape together with her…"

I don't remember how long their conversation was, and don't quite recall everything they said. For many years I could only recall certain parts of it. It wasn't until years later, when I finally located my mother's burial site on the outskirts of my hometown, that I suddenly remembered another bit: Father told Mother that he had been to our old house a few days earlier, and saw that the Germans still hadn't discovered the hideout, where there were supplies of food, water and blankets, enough for at least two weeks. He asked that if this coming Aktion proved not to be the final one, she would go hide back there, and he would join her later on. He said that if for whatever reason she couldn't make it to the old hideout, she should join our relatives the Klurmans, and together they would all escape to the village of Dovzhyk. There, in a secluded house at the heart of the forest, lived a family of Christians who were good friends with the Klurmans and had even received a large portion of their property as a gift.

But that memory only came to me fifty years later, as I walked down the old, death-ridden roads of Kamin retracing my family's final journey step by literal step. I was accompanied by an elderly gentile man who had led me up to the exact spot in the forest where they were buried.

Father and I Look for Shelter in the Surrounding Villages

Father must have agreed to Mother's request, because he took my hand, and we left the basement without looking back.

We walked the streets in broad daylight, like free, ordinary people. It had been three whole months since the last time I'd walked those streets and seen them with my own eyes. Now I could finally look around and enjoy the warm, sunny day and the clear, fresh air as it softly brushed our faces. Mother had dressed me up in two outfits that consisted of two dresses and two pairs of white socks. After that, she carefully combed my hair back into two long braids. Father wrapped himself in fur made of sheep wool and wore a jacket underneath. We headed towards the ghetto's main gate and walked out into the open. That was the first time I had actually gone through that gate. I had seen it so many times before, but no one was ever allowed to leave the ghetto. Those who were, did so only by direct order, only with a move permit, and only under the escort of a German officer.

But on that day, my last day in the ghetto – which would also be the last for any Jews therein who had managed to stay alive up to that point – it was suddenly allowed. I was overjoyed. It felt like I had been given a gift. Father and I, escaping the ghetto, walking together under the clear azure sky, with the sun blessing us by casting a beautiful glow upon the world.

I thought about the separation from Mother. I told myself we would probably be together again soon; after all, we didn't kiss, we didn't hug, we didn't even speak that much. She made sure to dress me up and get me prepared for leaving. She was probably aware of Father's plan to bring me over to their gentile friend but didn't say a word about it. She only repeated the words she had said to Father earlier… "You take Mashinka and escape with her."

Once we passed through the gate, we started marching briskly. I trusted Father and had complete faith in him. He always knew what to do and had always saved us all. I assumed he was planning to get to the forest and from there to the partisans whom I had heard so much about. I also knew that my eighteen-year-old cousin Aba Klurman had joined a unit of partisans and was fighting the Germans. But Father turned in a different direction, to his hometown of Verkhy, whose residents had known him since he was a boy. Along the way we passed by the train station and came across sixteen-year-old Lemma Klurman, another one of my cousins, and Father offered him to join us. The three of us continued making our way to the forest together. We walked for hours, and only at dusk did we arrive at the outskirts of the village and see the first of its houses. Father knew most of the locals and was convinced he would be able to find a solution there.

The next few days, however, taught us otherwise. For six days and nights we tried our luck, going door to door – a man, an adolescent boy and a young girl – and nothing. The cold of November was very much in full swing, and the chilling wind easily permeated our layers of clothes. The locals had been lighting their hearths to keep warm inside their homes, and we prayed one of them would open their door to us. We ached to get warm and rest, and to eat something, too. I was so hungry I had a stabby feeling in my stomach. But our prayers were not answered. The occasional passersby would throw us a slice of bread just to get us to go away. Father, determined as always, refused to give up. He waited until dark and then took us into one of the courtyards we'd passed by earlier, and from there into a sawmill or a barn of sorts. We fell exhausted onto the bales of hay, closed our eyes, and enjoyed a temporary respite. We stayed there for the following day, and come evening, when it seemed everyone had returned to their homes, we once again tried asking the villagers for help. But time and time again we were met with the same hostile response: having the door slammed in our faces and being explicitly ordered to leave.

Not a single door opened for us, and Father slowly came to the realization that the help he had hoped for would not come from the gentiles who had once been his friends. When we had left the ghetto a few days prior, we were confident that we would find a place to stay and leave the misery of the ghetto behind. After almost a week of one cold refusal after another, however, Father was starting to doubt our chances to survive – perhaps he had even lost hope altogether and given up, but I didn't know as much. On Saturday morning, we reached a house still under construction. There weren't any people around, and Father said it belonged to a man named Kravchuck.

The path we were walking down was surrounded by a thick forest stretching as far as the eye can see. It continued up to the town of Verkhy, about twenty kilometers away from Kamin. We easily climbed into the house and found a quiet spot to rest. We didn't have much food left, and the bread we had filled our pockets with had also run out. Father likely realized that the world he knew was forever gone and would never be the same again. He discovered he didn't have any friends left to rely on, and probably knew by then that the future ahead of us was uncertain and scary. I clung close to him, put my head by his chest and listened in to what he was going to say. I realize today that he was trying to prepare me for the new life that I was about to be thrust into. "You're a wise girl," he said. "You are smart and astute, and you know how to handle yourself. And you will. We have relatives around the world... In America, Argentina, and in the Land of Israel. I have buried a box with money in our yard."

"Here, I have even drawn you a map showing exactly where we are now, where it is hidden, and precisely where Kravchuck's house is." Father talked non-stop, repeating the same words over and over for the rest of the day. He tried his hardest to embed them deep into my brain and make me understand that the inevitable, the fateful moment we had been afraid of, was indeed happening. As I stood there, I listened while also not listening at all; let the words through while at the same time shutting them out, understood what Father was telling me while also not understanding a thing. I refused with all my heart and soul to recognize the reality he was building up towards.

"You're a smart girl", says Father. "I love you. You know how much I love you. You need to live, and we have relatives, and we are not alone." The hours passed and the darkness of early evening came along, descending upon the treetops and onto the road below. Father looks into my eyes and says... "Do you remember the woman you refused to go live with before? You know her. She lives not far from here, right at the end of this road, and she has promised me that if the worst came to pass, and if I ever had to be separated from you for some time, she would happily take you in as her own. And here we are now, close to her home…"

I remember he said… "Lemma and I will head down in a few moments, because we have to return home for Mother and see what happened in the ghetto. We need to see if Mother needs help. But don't worry, I promise to stay alive and come back for you, even if it takes a little time. You also have a cousin in the partisans, and you've got the information about our other relatives. You know many things that will help you manage without me. You will succeed, and you will live. After we jump, you will follow us down and along the lane." He then added… "See this jacket I'm wearing… It's for you. Inside its lining I've concealed photos of the entire family."

Father's jacket was packed with plenty of photos. It was as if the photo album we had at home was transferred in its entirety into the jacket. We spent the next hour looking through all the photos together. Who's this and who's that… Each person had a name, and each was a part of my family, past and present. Father took off his jacket and said to me… "Here, wrap yourself up in this and it will shield you from the cold. And most importantly, don't lose the photos. And near the edges, patched into the lining, is some money you might need." I did as he said and put on the heavy jacket. Since I wasn't as big as Father, some of the photos had to be taken out. He took them out of the pockets and hid them between the ceiling and the attic floor, to collect them in the future when he is able to come back.

Once we were done getting set up, Father said the woman, a gentile, lived approximately five kilometers away, just at the end of the road. He also said our town Kamin was approximately twenty-two kilometers away. "When we head down, you jump," he repeated once again. I can't recall if he told me to go on my own or said he would escort me to her.

Looking back, I realize that I understood nothing that day. Through all the talking, the explanations, the hours upon hours Father spent repeatedly explaining to me again and again what was going to happen, I wasn't really there with him. Throughout the entirety of that long day, I didn't even ask a single question. Perhaps I didn't believe him. Perhaps I didn't want to believe. We had already been through so much in that terrible year, and we always stayed together. So why now? Why did we suddenly have to separate?

"Jump", he said… "and after you land, stand up straight and start walking. Make sure to only walk to the left and not veer to the right. It will have gotten dark by then, and you'll be able to see stars in the sky. There's a series of telegraph poles stretching from here all the way up to her house. Walk right alongside them, pay close attention to their buzzing and you'll make it safely to her house." Father reiterated the woman's name and surname over and over, and what her house looked like from the outside. However, it was only when he and my cousin Lemma suddenly jumped into the darkness – practically lunging towards it – that I was finally hit with the stark realization of everything he had been telling me. It was like I had come out of a deep dream, and everything that had been asleep within me suddenly awoke in outcry.

Father had left me, alone, in the darkness of the forest!

10 *Alone Without Father*

I will never forget that moment. That terrible abandonment. And how I didn't even know Father and Lemma had been talking among themselves about jumping off and disappearing into the darkness. Words cannot describe how mad I was at him, how hurt I was, how insulted and miserable I felt for letting him do this to me. I knew he loved me with every fiber of his being; he had always instilled such a great sense of confidence in me. Always embracing me in his arms and telling me stories. And now he just leaves me here, all alone in this dark, scary forest, forcing me to survive on my own.

I was not even eleven years old at the time. I couldn't comprehend why he would suddenly leave. I couldn't accept his actions. I couldn't believe – and didn't want to believe – that Father would tell me, "you're going to have to be on your own, do things on your own, grow up on your own." I know he had been repeating those scary words over and over the entire day, but the instant he was out of my sight, everything went black, and I couldn't understand what had just happened. Nothing made sense. His many words all became disjointed in my head. Events from the past week and from the weeks before all became scrambled in my flooded mind… Images of Grandma, my brothers, Mother, the ghetto, I couldn't connect one thing to another, all I knew was that I was at the heart of the forest, abandoned and alone, with no one to hug me or hold me close.

I stood on the edge of the structure Father had jumped from a few seconds earlier. It was about three meters above ground, which made for a very scary sight. I told myself I had to do what Father said. The sky was still lit by the last few remaining traces of daylight, allowing me to see the path ahead, with the trees covering the countryside and the telegraph poles along the way. In my panic, a fearful shout came out of my throat: "Father… Father…" but he didn't answer. Perhaps he couldn't hear me by then, or perhaps he just hurried to get away. I realized at that moment that I had to get moving. I had to act as per Father's instructions and do what he'd been preparing me for. My temples were ringing and pounding, and my legs were trembling. I, Mashinka, was all alone out here in this forest, as night was beginning to descend upon it. I knew children were not supposed to be out in the woods by themselves after dark; Grandma would always tell me frightening stories about thick, dark forests with howling wolves, where all kinds of terrible things could happen. And now, as this big forest was being rapidly engulfed by the darkness of night, becoming full of strange and unfamiliar sounds, it seemed like it was going to swallow me whole at any moment.

I jumped down into the chasm below, just as Father and Lemma had earlier. When I landed, I immediately stood up straight like Father said, and listened for the faint, monotone buzzing of the telegraph poles. I started to walk, making sure to keep to the left. My eyes adapted to the darkness right away, and I used them to locate the poles. I had to put my arms out to the sides in order to touch them and not accidentally stray off the path. I didn't cry, I didn't make a sound, but my arms and legs were consumed by anxiety and fear, and my heart was beating intensely. With my fingers I felt for the photos in my pockets, constantly making sure they were still there and hadn't gone anywhere. The jacket covered my entire body and went nearly all the way down to my feet. As I kept walking, I slowly became more and more focused on the mission at hand, gradually coming out of the shock that had taken hold of me and concentrating on doing what Father had tasked me with.

The telegraph poles did indeed lead me right up to the entrance of the sawmill owned by Father's friend. I remembered her well from her repeated visits to our home in the ghetto, and I knew that Father greatly cherished her and had much faith in her. If he decided to put me in her care, I told myself, he must have known what he was doing.

The woman who opened the door recognized me instantly. I didn't have to say a single word. She warmly welcomed me inside and was kind and soft just like Father had promised. That only lasted for the first few minutes though, and after an hour she began to act just like all other people we had approached over the past week. She went outside and told her husband and their neighbors that I was there looking for a home or shelter. They immediately disapproved, telling her she mustn't take me in, warning her that the Germans would hurt her and her family, possibly even kill her. She initially tried to tell me that Father had written her a letter telling her not to take me in, but I didn't believe her and asked to see the letter. All the anger and hurtful feelings that had been boiling up inside me over the past few days, the fatigue and disillusionment, now came bursting out: the escape from the ghetto, the villagers' refusal to help us, Father's sudden and unexpected departure…

"Never mind what your father did or didn't say," she said. "I don't care if he wrote a letter or didn't write a letter, I don't need you here and I don't care about you, so leave now!"

I begged her to at least let me stay until morning. I was just so tired of everything and was all out of strength. She reluctantly agreed but made it clear that in the morning I would have to leave and never return.

The next morning, she handed me a bottle of tea and some bread and then promptly threw me out. It had been exactly one week since I separated from Mother and Moisha'le, and last night was the first without Father by my side. There I was, once again at the start of both a new week and a new period in my life, with no clue as to what I was supposed to do. From here on out, I thought, the only one I had left is me.

The feeling of loneliness burned in my face, burning my skin and gnawing away at my heart. I am a child all alone. A child without a father or a mother. A child without a family. A child without a home. A child unwanted. And I have to keep walking, but I don't know where to. Everything around me is threatening and scary. And the people are hostile and hateful towards me. And I'm not even eleven years old.

11 *Without a Home or Shelter*

I began walking through the forest, heading back to town. It had only been a week since I walked this path with Father, full of confidence, and now I'm going back without him. It's not like I had much of a choice. I prayed in my heart that the ghetto was still standing and that Mother and Father were down there in the basement. It was early in the morning, and coachmen from the surrounding villages occasionally passed by. They were headed for Kamin, possibly to ransack all the Jewish property left there, which was now up for the taking. Those who noticed me would stop their horses for a moment to shout insults and profanities my way. Everyone knew about the Jew girl wandering these parts all by herself. Some of the passersby spat my way, and some even hit me. Again and again I heard them say… "There goes the little Jew… Soon they'll kill you too…"

Not a single person offered to take me with them on their coach or asked where I was headed. Even so, I still tried asking for a favor, simply because of how badly I wanted to get to the ghetto already. I was exhausted, my legs were hurting, and I hoped Father and Mother were there waiting for me. But anyone I approached just shoved me off them blurting out obscenities. It went on like that for a whole day. They kept spitting and shoving, flailing their arms and occasionally hitting me – some even with a coachman's whip – to make sure I knew I had no place in their world.

By the time I reached the outskirts of town, my body was bruised and hurting, I was hungry and thirsty and the many tears rolling down my cheeks almost made me give up. The people I met all seemed evil and cruel and I didn't know what to do. The sun was about to set. After twenty kilometers, my legs could barely carry me anymore, and the only thing keeping me going was how desperately I wanted to get back to the ghetto and get a reprieve from the pain.

Along the way, I crossed another sawmill. The entire region was heavily forested, and there were several sawmills operating in the vicinity. I was familiar with the place. It was close to the outskirts of town – just a kilometer or two away from the ghetto I was so desperate to reach. To my horror, I saw German soldiers and some civilians turning over one plank after another. What are they doing, I wondered to myself. They must be looking for Jews; they're always looking for Jews. "No, I'm not going to fall right into their hands, not now", I told myself, and immediately turned back and fled the scene.

I had made it all that way for nothing. Something inside of me told me not to stay there. Not to stay there under any circumstances, no matter what. As soon as I had the opportunity, I got off the main road and on a side path going out of the sawmill and into another village named Puzyri (Ukrainian: Пузири) which, up until that point, I never knew existed, and whose name I had never heard. I also didn't know it would turn out to be one of the most horrific places I'd ever end up in.

On the one hand, my entire body was on edge for the faintest of sounds and the slightest of noises, but on the other hand, I was so weak and frightened. I so badly ached for some rest, for sleep, for a bit of human warmth. I went from house to house, knocking on the doors and windows with small fists so that people would see me and take pity. "Please," I said, "someone please, let me in and give me a slice of bread, let me get warm inside, I'm very cold." Though it hadn't started snowing yet, the cold of November was getting harsher and harsher. My feet were wounded and bruised and could barely take another step. I knocked on at least ten different doors, all shuttered and closed shut, and they all denied me with bitter cursing. Some would occasionally throw me a slice of bread in a moment of compassion, but none opened their door to me. The hatred had already consumed all. it was blatant and plainly visible, and the faces gazing down on me from the windows expressed either indifference or outright schadenfreude.

But I couldn't give up. I had to keep going. I continued going door to door, begging people to let me inside. Then, to my surprise, one door opened. Someone grabbed the handle and the door opened wide. Before me stood a hulking giant, enormous in size and completely drunk, examining me top to bottom with mad, glassy eyes. He grabbed me by the waist, lifted me up with one arm, and started throwing me up against the wall as if I were a ball. He throws, I fall on my knees and immediately get up, he grabs me and throws again, I get up again and he slams me into the wall – and so it goes on and on nonstop. Within minutes, the rumor about the captured Jew girl spreads throughout the village, and many people gather around us enthusiastically to witness the sadism. Drunk out of his mind and thrilled by the attention he was getting, the giant turned to me and said: "Now choose how you want to die… Should I choke you?" he asked, "…Burn you? Hang you? Or just throw you…?!"

And before I could think, a tin can full of crude oil was already being passed among the people.

In those few seconds of everyone gathering around and calling for my execution, I suddenly came out of the state of numbness I had been in, and without knowing where I'd heard it before, I answered: "I heard the Germans were giving away cigarettes for each Jew you bring them. Why don't you take me to the city tomorrow, bring me to them and they'll give you some?" Maybe it was the fact I suddenly spoke up that made everyone go quiet. The drunk giant answered, "Fine. I'll take you to the Germans." At that moment, he noticed the water bottle sticking out of my jacket pocket. "What's this," he thundered. "Could you also be a partisan?" I took advantage of the pause and answered in the voice of a person with nothing to lose: "Of course I'm a partisan, and I won't tell you where all the others are…"

"Yes, you will!" he roared, even though I knew he knew I was lying. He then went back to throwing me up in the air and against the wall like before, and I kept resisting, until he suddenly stopped.

"You eat pork?" he asked, seemingly out of nowhere…

"No", I said, "and you will not make me eat it, either. You're going to kill me tomorrow anyway, so I won't start eating pork now…"

"Yes, you will" he said, and I once again said no and continued to resist with all my might – but before I could say another word, he called in four other thugs just like him and said, "you will right now!", upon which he dragged me into one of the nearby homes, where the four of them held me down on a table by my arms and legs as he stood above me and forcefully shoved a hunk of pork meat in my mouth.

After that it's all a blank. I fell asleep. I didn't have any strength left to resist or to even be. Everything inside me had shut down, gone quiet and drifted off into the silence of a liberating, restorative slumber. And then, in my sweet and rejuvenating sleep, I saw Grandma – Grandma whom I loved very, very dearly. I said to her, "Grandma, do you know what they did to me, they held me down forcibly and made me eat pork." Grandma stroked me softly. "I know everything, my sweet child", she said. "Know that I am always watching over you." After that, I was awakened by the sound of loud banging on the window, with Grandma's kind words still pleasantly stroking my cheeks.

The giant was standing there. "Get up, come out, we're going to the city!", he yelled towards me. I knew from all the cursing of the day prior that all the Jews had been murdered. That everyone was dead. That the ghetto was completely vacant, without a single living soul. I knew Father and Mother were not there anymore. I thought maybe I should offer him the money Father had given me in exchange for my freedom, but I knew he would never let me go. I was exhausted, wounded and bruised, and all I wanted to do was close my eyes for a little longer and dream about my beloved Grandma. But I got up, came outside, and followed him to the city.

And yet, something inside of me, a tiny ember of will, still burned bright and refused to give out. I surveyed my surroundings to get a quick estimation of where I was. On the right was the road leading to town, and on the left was the main road leading to the village. He noticed I was distracted and told me to hurry up. I didn't respond, pretending I didn't hear him. He raised his voice and yelled at me, and I was still weighing my options, trying to figure out what to do. I continued to pretend not to hear him and began walking right in the opposite direction.

What happened next I cannot explain, but within seconds I found myself surrounded by about ten large dogs, all just as tall as I was, forming a circle around me. They growled loudly – but didn't bark – and kept close to me. I was almost completely obscured by them as they encircled me, practically serving as a protective belt shielding me from the outer world, as if to prevent all access to me. All the while, Grandma's words echoed over and over in my head… "I'm watching over you, I'm watching over you, I'm watching over you…" I continued walking with the dogs surrounding me, escorting me, and as I advanced further and further, I gradually stopped hearing the drunk giant's shouting and cursing as everything got farther and farther away from me. The village, the houses, the trees, the people. Finally, the group of canines disbanded and went its way, and I continued getting further and further away from there.

But where to..?! Returning to the city would be pointless, I knew that much. It was a Monday morning. At the end of the road would be my father's village, which I had left just the morning prior. This time around, fewer coaches came down the road, and those that did, mostly showed no interest in me. They ignored me and didn't even look. When the first few homes were within my sight, I went around the sawmill I had been forced out of before, and turned to look for assistance or for any sort of compassion among the other homes in the region. I knew that my family was well-known and held in high regard in this place; Grandpa was the owner of a large windmill, and everyone in town respected him and benefited from his services in one way or another.

I told myself that someone was bound to eventually take me in, that there had to be someone who would care, that I only had to find one family. I knocked on door after door, yelling: "I am Masha Drajcen, Grandpa Drajcen's granddaughter, Zelig Drajcen's daughter. You must know who I am." But just like in the week prior, not a single door opened, and no one invited me inside their home for a little bit of rest. The occasional passerby would throw me a slice of bread, both so that I wouldn't starve and so I'd go away.

As time went on, the days blended together. Night and day mixed with each other, without shelter, food, or the consolation I so badly needed. I wanted so much to just sit by a hearth and get my frozen palms warm. I longed so much for the interior of a home, for a table and chair, for a mug and a plate, for water to wash my dirty face with, for clean clothes, even for someone to just speak to me, just a single word. At night I would stealthily enter one of the barns or pig pens in the area without being noticed to find a safe spot where I could put my head down.

Just three weeks ago I still had a home, and siblings, and parents who deeply cared for me.

One night, I went inside a pig pen. Though I was scared of the pigs, I knew the inside the pen would be warmer and safer than outside. In the dead of night, I heard some faint voices. It was a small group of partisans, heading out of the forest to scavenge for food. I wanted so much to approach them and tell them I'm Jewish, to ask if maybe they could take me with them to the forest, and maybe even bring me to my cousin who was also there. But I dared not stand up and reveal myself. I regretted it a thousand times afterwards and kept wondering if they would have taken me with them and kept me safe. It was a moment of confusion, uncertainty, and great stress, and within mere seconds they'd already passed the pen and disappeared into the night, along with any opportunity I might have had.

I came out of the pen and noticed the light was on in one of the houses. I gently knocked on the door, and to my surprise, it opened, and I was invited inside. They sat me down on a chair and served me a warm glass of milk. the first glass of milk I'd had in many days. It was like a miracle, like a sweet dream I wished would last forever. I went to sit by the hearth, submerging myself in its heat as it enveloped me from head to toe. For a moment I was a real child; a real child in a different world. They talked among themselves about the partisans roaming the region, and showed me sympathy and compassion. Once my body got warm and my hunger somewhat sated, I went out and continued walking, with no clear direction or thought as to where to go. From time to time, I would come across bales of hay that had been left out in the fields, and crawl under them to get a pleasantly warm temporary shelter from both the cold and the ever-present sense of fear in the air. I made sure to stick to the primary roads, because I was afraid of getting lost in the vast stretches of forest. Under the protective cover of the bales of hay, I would find relief from the constant tension and allow a deep sleep to come over me, or I'd get absorbed in pleasant thoughts about Father, about how we're both probably looking for each other; about the possibility that I'd find him someplace and then we would all unite and be a family again.

12 *Over the Next Few Weeks...*

My entire way of life had changed drastically compared to anything I'd known before. I didn't bathe, didn't change clothes, and didn't brush my hair. I became riddled with lice and dirt and was no longer the child I had once been. My body was itching, my head was itching, I was covered in scratches and wounds, and just felt awful overall. I was certain I had traveled enormous distances. though In reality I had been walking in circles, passing through the same villages over and over again.

One day, I was approached by a horse-drawn coach. A gentile coachman called out to get my attention. "Come on up", he said. "Everyone around here knows about the Jew walking around here, the little girl, Drajcen's granddaughter..." I immediately got on the coach, after which he said, "I'm bringing you to a village of "Shtundists". They'll keep you safe."

I had never heard that word before and had no idea who those "shtundists" were. I know today that it's a small, separatist Christian sect whose members are prohibited from ever inflicting harm upon another, as well as from standing idly by when they can save others from harm.

We arrived at a village by the name of Karpilovka. The coachman brought me to the head of the village, who willingly let me inside his home, served me a plate of warm and tasty soup – a gesture not to be taken for granted in my situation – and sat me down to have a conversation. He was a highly respected man within his community, and I was a dirty, abandoned, hungry child, riddled with wounds and lice and wearing worn-out rags. He presented me with a Christian Bible and asked if I knew what it was. I told him I didn't, upon which he began telling me numerous stories from the New Testament. I was as opinionated and stubborn back then as I was young and foolish, and immediately dismissed everything he said, insisting I had only ever heard about the stories of the Hebrew Bible. I knew there was a Jesus, but I also knew it was something forbidden and off-limits, something untrue. With zero hesitation, I rejected his words and refused to accept anything he said. For about two hours he tried and tried to convince me of the truth of his stories, but I remained steadfast in my naysaying and refused to accept them. Why, just this past year, Father had hired a tutor to teach me and Moisha'le the stories of the Hebrew Bible, and everything was still very fresh in my memory. The New Testament, however, I had never heard of before.

And then he added… "You know what… if you want us to take you in and rescue you, you need to accept our faith." I seem to recall his voice being pleasant and soft and his words being fair and considerate, even implying he would stay out of whatever I chose to believe in my heart of hearts. He did say, however, that outside, in public, I would have to choose their way, and not identify as Jewish.

Yet I, despite all the hurdles I had been through, and with the confidence of a ten-and-a-half-year-old who knew exactly what was the right thing to do in these types of situations, said, "Absolutely not. If I have to die, I'll die as a Jew," and without a second thought, adamantly rejected his generous offer. He looked me regretfully in the eye and said, "I am very sorry, but I will not be able to help you", upon which he sent me on my way.

Anastasiya, My Good Samaritan

13

I left his home and started walking towards the other houses scattered throughout the area, all of which were in fact Shtundist homes. Nighttime was approaching, and I used my eyes to scan for a spot where I'd be able to put my head down until the next morning. Once again, I began knocking on the village doors asking for shelter. Having been by myself for about a month at that point, I had completely mastered the Ukrainian language, and people understood precisely who I was and what I was asking for. My neglected, beggarly appearance also made it clear beyond a shadow of a doubt: a Jewish girl wandering the streets and forests all on her own, looking for a place to sleep and eat. And as always, people's doors remained shut.

I continued making my way through the village until I reached one of the last houses. Daylight was all but gone, with only a mere few shadows still visible on the ground. I knocked on the door, upon which a woman emerged from the house, approached me and said, "I know who you are. Wait here, don't go anywhere. I will be free to let you inside in a few moments."

I sat on a big rock and waited.

As the dark cover of night began its timely descent, so too did the loneliness and cold I had gotten used to over the past few months. Some old man from a nearby hut passed me by and started asking me questions. I answered willingly at first, but then decided against it – that it would be best not to say a word – and closed off to him. I prayed that the woman would come out as she had promised and let me inside her home, away from all those people whose intentions I didn't know. Just then, she quietly appeared, grabbed my arm, and pulled me inside. "I have a daughter exactly your age", she said. "I can't imagine what she'd be going through if, Heaven forbid, she had to do what you've been doing. You can stay here for a day or two, get warm and get your strength back, and once you're better, I'll see what I can do. But no one can know you're here", she added sternly. "I have a Ukrainian teacher living in my home, and she must never find out about you, or she might rat you out."

She looked at me as if wondering what was the most pressing thing I needed.

"First make the itching go away", I told her.

"That would mean I'd have to cut off your braids", she said.

"Okay, cut them off", I replied.

And thus she cut off my braids – the braids Mother had combed for one last time just before I left the ghetto – and wrapped them in paper. Many years later, when I met with her daughter Vaska, she told me that her mother had kept them with her all through the war.

She gave me some clean clothes of her daughter's to change into, and took my own dirty clothes to wash. She took Father's jacket and put it away. She then led me into a large room, at the center of which stood a type of hearth which she called a "Rus'ka Pich (Ukrainian: Руська піч, meaning. "Russian Stove")", which resembled a double bed and was kept burning all through the winter. Its upper surface was large enough to sleep on and was always nice and warm. Though the room had neither flashlights nor any electric or petroleum-fueled light sources, the twigs burning in the hearth filled the area with a soft, soothing glow amidst the darkness.

I fell asleep in an instant. My sleep was wonderful that night; my body was bathed in a feeling of peacefulness and warmth and drifted into a deep, curative slumber. The following morning, she began to think about what to do with me moving forward. At the first light of dawn she wrapped me up in rags and a blanket to keep me warm, and led me into a small pantry stocked with goods. She warned me to keep completely silent. "You can't make so much as a sound", she said. "you must stay quiet." The pantry was practically located outside, like a shed separate from the house. Its walls had a few cracks in them which made it possible to watch what was happening outside, while no one from the outside could see what was happening inside. "I'll keep you closed off in here for now", she told me, "and see what else I can do… You'll have to wait until the evening to relieve yourself, because you can never go outside during the day; God forbid anyone should see or hear you and become suspicious."

From then on, I'd spend the days in the pantry and only come out at night. The pantry was dark throughout the day, with very little light slipping in from the outside. At the center was a large, table-like crate I could sit or lie on. Her words echoed in my mind… Don't make a sound… And I abided by them religiously, never even moving around the room. I had absolute self-discipline, and not even the faintest of noises ever came from the pantry. I would spend most of my time there dreaming and conjuring things up in my mind or setting up tasks for myself to achieve. The first was to hone my sense of hearing. I told myself that in case Father or my partisan cousin Aba Klurman happened to pass by the house, I had to be able to hear and recognize their voice.

Every day I would spend hours listening to all kinds of noises, voices and sounds from the outside: birds, people, gusts of wind, raindrops falling on the ground, footsteps, coaches passing by, whispers of morning, nights in their descent. Afterwards I'd come up with plans on how to pass the days, trying to find activities I could perform without moving any part of my body – not even my arms and legs – or creating as much as a faint ripple in the air. I'd fix my eyes on the ceiling, reciting in my heart every song and poem I knew. After that, I'd do counting and calculation exercises; I'd count up to a thousand or a million, for instance, and if I made the unfortunate mistake of losing count, I'd start again from that point and continue on.

After that, I'd draw up all kinds of shapes in the air: triangles, circles, big and small, upward and downward… I spent days upon days not letting out a single word – not needing words – keeping my promise to stay silent and make sure no one knew of my existence.

The most captivating daydreams were the ones about reuniting with Father. I'd dream about him suddenly arriving out of nowhere to surprise me. I wasn't sure I'd be able to tell him what I'd been through since we separated. I focused on how he'd hug me, what he'd say to me, and what had happened to him since, and how Mother was doing. I wanted so badly to feel his hug, to relish in a soothing touch and loving words. I wanted him to be proud of me for having managed to live just as he had reiterated to me over and over when we separated so long ago. I wanted him to see that he was right, that I truly was the smart and capable girl he said I was.

Days in the pantry were all more or less the same. I did just as my goya had instructed, not letting out a single sound. I didn't even move. I became almost invisible. I felt I was a heavy burden on her shoulders. My stay made her very fearful, and it was practically every day that she'd say to me – and to herself – "what am I going I do with you?! If I send you away, the Germans will kill you before the day is out," to which I'd quietly reply, "whatever you decide, I will do."

Aside from her, only her two children knew I was hiding in the pantry: her daughter Vaska, who was the same age as me, and her son Pavluk, who was about fourteen. Pavluk didn't like the fact I was staying with them, and hardly ever tried to converse or exchange any words with me. Sometimes on Sundays, when my goya went out to church, he would come into the pantry, beat me up, and warn me to say nothing to his mother – which, of course, I never did.

One night, my ears picked up unusual sounds. I'd greatly sharpened my hearing by then, and had learned to pick up even the faintest of noises. I was able to make out that those sounds were voices of people talking. Somehow I knew in my gut that it was the partisans, raiding the village for food and supplies. Granted, the Germans would raid villages sometimes too, but never under the guise of darkness, and never in such a cautious silence.

The villages were no longer being actively searched for Jews at that point, as it was quite clear to everyone that there weren't any living Jews left. No one knew about me, of course. My goya said that even the head of the village wondered where I had disappeared to. Everyone said it was as if I'd been swallowed by the earth.

On another night, as I was basking in the warmth of the hearth, the Ukrainian teacher suddenly returned home earlier than expected. This caught me and my goya completely off-guard. Before we had time to recover from the shock, she had already climbed up on the Rus'ka Pich to get warm. I didn't know what to do; I didn't know what I was expected to do. Everything happened so fast and I just froze in place, desperately trying to hold my breath, preparing myself for the worst. My goya immediately leaped to her feet, rushed to put out the light coming from the twigs in the hearth, darkened the room completely, climbed up on the Rus'ka Pich as well, and lay down right on top of me to make sure I wasn't discovered. She was somewhat of a larger woman, and I was a fragile little girl. I could barely breathe, and though I tried my damnedest not to make a sound, a small squeak escaped my throat.

"What was that?" the teacher asked, taken aback by the sudden beep.

"Oh, that's our sick cat. I brought it up here. It is very sick; you should be careful around it", said my goya.

The Ukrainian teacher finally gave up and went off to her room. My goya and I finally refilled our lungs with air and breathed a long sigh of relief, though the feeling of anxiety and panic lingered in our hearts long after.

On a different night, the Germans came without notice and surrounded the village. Though they weren't looking for Jews, they were hunting down partisan

An Ukrainian Rus'ka Pich

collaborators in partisan-loyal villages. They also used these raids as opportunities to replenish their food supply, by forcefully taking food away from the villagers. Sometime around dawn, a German soldier suddenly entered the house. Though I knew the Germans were in the village, I couldn't get to the pantry in time. My goya had warned me that they were searching the area: "If they find you", she said, "I'm not here and I don't know anything about you", to which I said: "Okay." I had heard enough times that if the Germans ever found out someone was harboring Jews, they would kill them, too. Her son Pavluk would tell me over and over that they would all end up dead because of me.

And then the door suddenly opened, and a German soldier in a well-pressed military uniform and immaculately polished shoes stood at the entrance, right in front of me. There was no way I could have found a hiding spot in time. To climb up the hearth, which was about a meter-and-a-half tall, I would have had to first get up on the bench and then jump onto the upper surface from there; it would have been like leaping two stairs at once.

The German stood on the bench and fixed his gaze upon me. I was trembling from top to bottom; my hands were trembling, my legs were trembling, and my teeth were chattering. But he didn't seem to notice the terror that had taken hold of me. He gave me a malcontent look and then yelled towards my goya: "What's this?" And she, who always showed amazing ingenuity, yelled back from outside, "Oh, that's... That's my daughter, she has typhus..." He got off the bench and left as he came, not giving me another look.

My mouth was dry. I couldn't stop trembling. This was the first time in a long time I had seen a German up-close. I was sure he'd kill me on the spot if he got suspicious even in the slightest, or if I made any sort of mistake.

Evenings such as that one, when the Germans raided a village in search for collaborators, also saw many partisans infiltrating the village and scavenging the fields and courtyards for food. One morning, unusual voices once again broke the regular silence of the pantry. Just like last time, before I could vanish into the darkness of the pantry, the door opened, and a young man entered the house. He pulled my goya into the other room and started asking her questions. Despite my best efforts, I couldn't make out what they were saying. And yet, something about his voice seemed familiar. And then it suddenly hit me: it was my cousin Aba Klurman, who had escaped into the forest before the ghetto was terminated! Somehow I just knew it was him. Before Father and I separated, he kept telling me over and over, "You have a cousin in the partisans." "Yes... It's his voice," I thought, barely able to contain my excitement. "Or maybe it isn't. Maybe I'm just imagining things and it's really someone else." In the end, I could no longer hold myself. The inner struggle became too much to bear. I so badly wished for it to be my cousin. I leaped off the Rus'ka Pich, entered the other room, and yes... The miracle I had been wishing and praying for had come true, right in front of my very eyes. Standing in that room was my cousin Aba Klurman – him and no other.

The instant I recognized him, I immediately jumped into his arms. It was an unbelievable moment. A miraculous scene that seemed like it was taken out of

My cousin Aba Klurman with his wife Sisel

a fairytale. For so long I had been on my own, alone, without a family. And now, my cousin is here with me, standing right there, and I can reach out and touch him, and get a hug and a kiss. He may have been eight years older than me – he was a young man, and I was just a small, lean-bodied child – but his being in the room filled me with hope and joy so great, it was as if I had found my entire family.

Before the war, I hardly ever saw him. He had already moved out of Kamin, and I was the age of his little sister. Whenever he blessed Grandma with a visit, I would observe him from afar: his perpetual smile, his dressing style, his blue eyes. I knew him simply as Grandma's beloved eldest grandchild.

And now he's here for me. A partisan warrior fighting back against the Germans. I couldn't be prouder, couldn't be happier. I was simply overjoyed. He carried a rifle, and I was wrapped in rags upon rags to shield me from the cold. The joy bursting out of me was so huge and granted me such relief that just for a moment, I could put aside my sadness and forget.

Aba Klurman informed me that all members of our family had been killed – murdered – in November of 1942.

My father Zelig and my cousin Lemma were murdered the very same night they parted ways with me in the forest. As for the other members of the family

72

– Aba Klurman's parents David and Menucha (my mother's sister), his siblings Masha, Shiye (Joshua) and Hershale (Herschel), my mother Freidel and my brother Moisha'le – though they managed to flee to the village of Dovzhyk, they were murdered by the locals shortly after they arrived there. He told me he arrived at Dovzhyk two days after the ghetto had been terminated in the final Aktion, and marked their burial site with a pole, so as to be able to locate it after the war.

Despite the tragic news and the terrible realization that my parents were never coming back, despite knowing that and all other members of my family were gone forever and that I couldn't continue having conversations with them in my mind anymore – the fact I had an actual relative with me, whom I could touch and hug and kiss, made me very emotional. I felt like a long-dormant volcano that was finally erupting. Copious amounts of love and light were bursting out of me, while at the same time copious amounts of love and light were flowing from him into me, filling the air I breathed with a newfound sense of vitality, and huge hope that would keep burning within me for days to come. That wonderful moment of meeting my cousin, and his loving hug, instantly restored my will to keep on living.

For years I believed that Aba Klurman had found me thanks to a relative of my goya's – her aunt – who came to visit her one day. It's likely my goya had been aching to share her secret with someone and get some encouragement and affirmation for her actions. "I have a little girl in the house," she said. "A Jewish girl. The one who people say has been swallowed by the earth. The one who even the head of the village keeps asking about ever since she walked out his door."

Amazingly, her aunt told her that she had been harboring a Jewish man in her home. "Ask the little girl to write a letter to him. It could be her father..." My goya rushed to tell me the news and asked me to write a letter detailing precisely who I was, where I was from and who my relatives were. I wrote down everything: the name of my hometown, the names of my mother and father and grandmother and grandfather. I knew that everyone in the area was familiar with my family, and prayed in my heart that I would not be alone anymore.

It was only many years later that I found out the truth: my letter never made it to my cousin. The circumstances of how he found me were completely different, and sound like something out of a fairytale, an unbelievable story, even by the standards of back then.

Being a partisan fighter, Aba Klurman had been to my goya's village many times prior. According to him, her house always attracted him somehow, though he couldn't put his finger on as to why. He also knew the Ukrainian teacher who lived there and believed her to be in contact with both the partisans and the Germans. The night before, when he returned from a partisan mission with a group of his comrades, they went to see a gypsy card reader. Seeking to unwind and get some respite, they agreed to have her tell them their fortunes. Aba Klurman didn't take the ordeal very seriously, but when his turn came, he agreed to cooperate all the same. To his surprise, she looked at him and said,"That house, the one you've been to before… Focus on it! You might find someone there who's close to you…"

Years later, in a conversation at which my daughter, Limor, was also present, he recalled: "I didn't really believe her, but I was so close to the house, I thought I might as well go there and check it out. The only person I could think of was my sister Golda, who I knew had managed to escape the ghetto before its termination. It never even crossed my mind that it could be you. I entered the house, and before I could even get through the pleasantries, you came out of nowhere and jumped at me!"

But Aba Klurman didn't take me with him. I stayed with my goya for a while longer, though I'm not sure by how much, or how the meeting ended. What I do remember is her telling me, "I'm so glad he found you. Now I won't be the only one taking care of you."

In the following days, I waited just for him. I knew the whole situation was hard on my goya – having to bear the responsibility of keeping me hidden at the risk of bringing disaster upon her family, constantly on alert for unexpected snitches. Before he left, my cousin assured her that he would find an arrangement and get me off her hands as soon as possible.

The next time the Germans raided the village, she said to me, "I can't deal with this anymore. I'm tired of this. I don't care about anything anymore. What am I going to do with you?!" She pulled me out of the house and led me to a dark storage room meant for storing potatoes, which had air flowing in from outside through a narrow hatch. It was a cold day in the winter of February 1943. Temperatures were running very low, and to make sure the cold didn't spoil the potatoes, my goya had brought in a batch of hot coals in a tin bucket to turn up the heat. I curled up next to the coals. Standing outside, she told me: "From now on, I don't know anything. There are Germans in the village, and I don't know what will happen to you and I." She concealed the hatch with a tin tub from the yard and went back inside.

I lay on the pile of potatoes in the storage room. The flow of air inside had become significantly limited due to the tub covering the hatch. The hot coals in the bucket made a cloud of smoke which gradually grew thicker and thicker, eventually making it impossible to see anything at all. I remained curled up near the bucket in a fetal position, making sure not to move, make any sound, or draw attention in the slightest.

My goya realized I might choke from the smoke; as the hours passed, she was certain I'd already run out of air, and began to think about where she would be able to bury me without anyone noticing. This went on for several hours, until eventually she became so utterly tormented by these haunting thoughts, so restless, that despite the terrible fear of what she might find, she rushed to the storage room to check on me. By then, I was lying unconscious under the hatch, close to suffocating on the smoke. If she hadn't entered and pulled me out, I would have certainly died that time.

It is thanks to my Anastasiya Gotsyk – my goya, as I called her – that I ultimately survived. She put a roof over my head, showed me kindness and compassion, tended to my wounded, aching body, and granted me a reprieve from all the hurdles I'd been through and all the hostile, hateful encounters with people who wanted me dead. Her protection gave me the time I needed to rest and recuperate in a quiet environment, and the strength not to give up. She gave me the opportunity to collect myself, to rest from all the evil lurking in the

Anastasiya Gotsyk

villages, from the murderous thugs, the piercing cold and the dark, scary nights. She took me in and restored my belief in good people. She fed me, cleaned me, got me out of the pantry and laid me to sleep on the Rus'ka Pich every night, and helped me back into the pantry again every morning, just before everyone else woke up. She guarded me from others, exhibiting great courage in her choice to be different, to act in a world of inaction, to care in a world uncaring, all while risking her life and the lives of those closest to her. I knew she was thinking about me every minute of every day and living in constant fear, just as I was.

My goya harbored me for about four months, from December 1942 to March 1943. And then, when spring was around the corner, as the snow was beginning to thaw, a young partisan by the name of Arye Segal suddenly showed up at the house. He had been sent by my cousin Aba Klurman to finally take me to another safe haven. It was a moment of joy and relief both for myself and for my goya. She was genuinely excited for me when he came: excited by the fact that I had a family, that I had people looking out for me, that I would be raised among the people I was close to, and that perhaps I could stop hiding all the time.

Her name was Anastasiya Gotsyk, and she will forever and ever be my good Samaritan, the angel who saved me.

At the Partisan Camp in the Forest

14

I have no recollection of how I said goodbye to my goya, or of the long on-foot journey I hastily made with the partisan afterwards, all the way up to his group's remote camp at the heart of the forest. We crossed one of the tributaries of the Stokhid River. The weather was freezing that day, and no amount of clothing I put on was enough to shield me from the intense cold. As

we walked across a small bridge of a couple of rot wooden beams, I fell and got my legs wet with the icy water. Though I tried my hardest to keep up with the partisan, I found myself mostly stumbling after him.

About twenty other adults were also walking with us, and I was the only child in the group. The journey went on and on as we trudged through the night, and it was

Stokhid River in the winter

only around dawn that we finally arrived at the outskirts of the forest. It was near the city of Pinsk – very far away from Kamin-Kashirsky.

The forest stretched over a large area, and was lush and thick enough to be a viable hiding place from the Nazis and their collaborators. Various partisan groups had set up camp there, as well as civilian families who did not participate in the fighting but had escaped to the forest and lived under the support of the partisans.

Throughout the camp, the partisans had dug special diagonal dugouts called Zemlyanka (Russian or Ukrainian: Землянка, Polish: ziemianka), inside which people could hide from the intense cold. Each was about twenty meters long and had been dug half a meter deep into the ground, meaning they were tall enough for me to stand up straight in them. I seem to remember they were tall enough for most of the adults as well. Inside each Zemlyanki was a wooden bench wide enough to sleep on, and they became my new home.

Zemlyanka – a partisan shelter in the forest

As soon as we arrived at the forest, Arye Segal, the partisan who brought me, bid me farewell and went on his way. I didn't know any of the other people there, and despite having been yearning for the company of others, I still felt alone. Everything felt so unfamiliar and different, and the fact I had just spent months in complete silence and immobility made the change even more dramatic. Suddenly there was fresh air to breathe in again, and the sights and sounds of nature, and the voices of other human beings, among whom were even other children like me. I was free to move my legs as much as I wanted, walk around, discover new sights, speak, and once again be a curious child going about the world.

But in my heart of hearts I deeply missed my goya, who had been like a mother to me and was now no longer with me. I knew that If I hadn't met her that afternoon, if she hadn't taken me in, I undoubtedly would have died that day. The pantry where I hid during the day, the pleasant warmth of the Rus'ka Pich I slept on at night, the rags she'd wrap me in, the clothes she'd dress me in, and above all, her kind and generous heart…

Were it not for all those things, I would certainly have frozen to death somewhere out in the field or along the desolate roads – that is, if some raging villager didn't kill me first.

And now I am here, among people, all Jews who just like me have escaped deep into the heart of the forest, away from the hostile villages and the main roads. The members of the camp all seemed like fortified, hardened people.

They were reclusive and withdrawn, initiating little interaction with their peers. I didn't play or speak with the children either; I did not know what their names, where they had come from, if they had any relatives they'd left behind, what their lives had been like before the war, or what they had been through up until that point.

Fortunately for me, one of the couples at the camp, who had no children of their own, decided to take me under their wing and adopt me. They retreated from the other families and set up a small dugout at the edge of camp. I spoke to them in Yiddish, in conversations which were practically my first time speaking after months of not uttering a single word. I spoke to my goya in Ukrainian, but only when answering her questions. Aside from that, I had gotten used to being mute, nodding or shaking my head for a yes or a no; never making a sound, not even to laugh. I lived in complete silence, just as she had instructed.

But even here, in the company of other Jews like myself, my wall of loneliness did not break. I felt alone in the world, a little girl among strangers. Alone with my thoughts, alone with the time which dragged on and on from dusk to dawn. The hours turned into days and the days turned into weeks. Without a soul to lean on or anyone to belong with. Without the gentle touch of a loving hand, or a reassuring smile. No one asked me what my name was or who my family was, how I ended up in the forest or if I had any relatives or friends. It felt like no one even noticed I was there with them.

For the most part, our daily routine was always the same. The men would occasionally head out to the surrounding villages at night to raid them for food. In the spring of 1944, the balance of power in the frontier finally changed for the better, and the Russian army enjoyed many victories over the German forces. Having learned that the Russians had the upper hand and were advancing west, even the villagers who had been previously collaborating with the Germans understood that Axis Powers were headed towards defeat and would eventually be forced to retreat. Everyone now treated the partisans with reverence and respect, providing them with potatoes and bread, which made up the bulk of our diet since they were easy to carry during our nightly voyages.

In the entire time I stayed with my goya, I never had any meat. I told her on day one that I didn't eat meat. Maybe it was because I always suspected the meat she had could be pork, which I had a strong aversion to, since it was considered non-Kosher and strictly forbidden in Judaism. In the forest, however, pork was considered highly valuable since its fat could keep the body warm in the intense cold. At the end of winter, after the snow melted, we collected blueberries, wild mushrooms and other kinds of fruit and edible herbs.

One morning in the spring, a month or so after I arrived, the couple who had adopted me went to look for food. They did not return in the evening, or in the following day. Everyone at camp knew I was theirs and that they were providing for me. After a day or two, someone came looking for them in their dugout, and I told him they still hadn't returned. I told him what I knew: that I'd been waiting for them for the past two days. This immediately made everyone at camp very concerned for their fate. A group of men went out to scan the area, and found their bodies lying on the road. They had been shot dead. The men who found them said their bodies were rolled up on their stomachs, as if they'd been rolled over with a rolling pin.

I was on my own again. By then, however, I had assimilated into the larger group and had become a part of it. I'd been blessed with a new family, too. Elka Fuchs, a young woman whose boyfriend was a partisan in the same camp as my cousin Aba Klurman, and a couple of older parents whose son was also in the partisans. I was glad they knew who I was and had known my family before the war. I felt safe in their presence, and at night I would fall asleep right beside Elka, clinging to her as if she were my big sister.

During this time, the partisan resistance in the area was at its peak. Battles between the partisans and the German army took place on a daily basis. Not only did the partisans go after German soldiers, but they also used dynamite to blow up railways, preventing the Germans from transporting ammunition by train. We would hear about what was happening from partisans coming to visit us at camp. My cousin Aba Klurman couldn't visit me, but he made sure to regularly send me comforting little gifts. One such gift I remember especially well was an embroidered, long white gown made of cotton: it was too large for my size, so the woman who had adopted me sewed a remarkably beautiful dress out of it instead. For a moment, camp felt like a normal home. I did not have new shoes – my old ones had worn out and come apart – but it didn't matter anymore. Our hearts were full of newfound hope, and the good news from the frontier gave us strength; the dream of the war ending didn't seem so far out of reach anymore. Father's jacket – the brown one, with the velvet-like fur and the golden coins patched into its lining – was still with me. My goya had kept it for me. She understood how valuable it was and I didn't have to say a single word. She knew its pockets had photos of my entire family inside them; the same invaluable photos Father had given me just before we separated. When I left her, she gave it back to me along with all my other clothes, laundered and clean, and said… "The photos of your family are all in there. Of your aunts and uncles, and your mother and father, and your brother, and your Grandma..."

15 *A Raid on the Forest*

What little peace those days brought with them came to an abrupt end when rumors reached camp about someone having snitched on us. People were saying the Germans were going to raid the forest for partisans. Within mere seconds, a huge panic broke out, sending the entire camp into chaos. Everyone started running, and I followed, not waiting for Elka and my new family. I just started running as fast as I could, like everyone else. I just barely managed to grab my precious jacket before running in a panic after the others. I noticed they were getting the little children up on the horse-drawn coach from camp. I was tired from running; my feet were trembling from fatigue, and I felt like I was going to fall at any moment. I asked the coachman to let me up on the coach so I could have a moment's rest.

"I'm very tired", I begged. "let me up on the coach." But he shoved me off angrily, ignoring my plea. Angry, exhausted and confused, I took off Father's jacket, which up until that very moment I had been guarding with my life, threw it at the coach, and continued running without it. I kept running with all my might, passing one tree, and another, and another. All that running made me dizzy, so I stopped for a moment to lean against one of the tree trunks along the way. With blurry vision, I looked back and thought I could see a group of men on horses heading right for me; not German soldiers, but rather Ukrainian collaborators, who were going to catch up to me any second and murder me right then and there. When I came to and continued running, I realized the coach had continued without me and I was alone yet again.

When the darkness of the night descended upon the forest, I stopped running. It had been a difficult day, and night didn't bring with it any peace or respite. I arrived at a glade where I saw a woman with her two grown-up sons. There was no one else around aside from them. She had wrapped her children in a wool blanket to keep them warm. I tried asking her to let me cuddle in under the blanket with them, but she aggressively pushed me away. My entire body was aching with envy, aching from loneliness, aching to belong.

I was the child of no one.

When Father left me in that abandoned building to survive on my own, a sense of utter shock took over me. As the days passed, I learned to be alone. But on that night, everything fell into pieces. All of my bravery, all my power, all my will. The forest seemed thicker and more menacing than ever before. The people had never seemed more estranged. The stars had never seemed colder or farther away. My body was hurting in the chilling wind. And Father's jacket, which was given to me to instill a sense of safety and confidence in me, had been left up on the coach and I had no possible way of knowing where it could have ended up. I remained lying there until morning, curled up on the cold, hard soil, and didn't know how I could keep going.

By the time I woke up from my restless sleep, there was no one else around. No one could be bothered to wake me up and take me along with them. I hurried to my feet and started walking, looking for some indication of a nearby road or lane. I began to walk faster, looking to the sides to determine where to go. After a short while, I could see a house not too far away. Even in the more secluded and far-out parts of the forests, one could occasionally come across a house or farm intentionally built in the backwoods, away from people. I knocked on the door and walked inside. A person who appeared to be a farmer asked what I was looking for, where I had come from, and who my parents were. I knew he was Ukrainian since only Ukrainians lived in that area.

I explained that I was no one's child; that I was a child wandering the forest by herself, and that I was in desperate need of some rest. It turned out he was already harboring a family of Jews in his home. He asked them to look after me, and they adamantly refused. This angered him greatly, and he decisively said, "if that's how it is, if you really refuse to look after her, then I'll throw you out and let the girl take your place..." And indeed, he forced them out and let me inside his home in their stead.

I only stayed in his house for a mere few days. I needed to recuperate, to recover lost strength and let my freezing body get warmer so I could get back on my feet. Once I got a little better, he said to me: "I'm very sorry, but I can't keep harboring you any longer. He wrapped me up in a coat, sat me down under one of the trees in the forest, turned his back and walked away until I could no longer see him in the distance.

16 *An Angel in the Forest*

And so, just like before – just like countless times before – I was on my own. Alone. A child not twelve years of age, left out in the forest wrapped in a coat, leaning against the trunk of a tree; a child now all too familiar with the cold, the heavy silence of the forest, the deep loneliness. I felt there was no more hope. I have never given up until now, I told myself… I have never given in. I've done just what Father said. I wanted to live, and I did live. I did everything just the way Father said.

But now, something inside me was tired. The burden of the mission had become so heavy on my shoulders, it was just impossible to bear. My body was completely drained, and my dried-out heart all but burnt out. I curled up under the tree, hugged my body from underneath the coat with my tired hands, and fell into a slumber… Or fainted… Or perhaps it was just daydreaming…

Time became nothing, and I became detached from everything.

A few hours must have passed. It was late in the afternoon when some rustling noises pulled me out from the depths of a dream. I slowly opened my eyes and looked up. Right above me stood a remarkably beautiful young woman, with a pair of blue eyes examining me with a soft and curious look. It was a teenage girl, around seventeen or eighteen years old. She gently touched me and began asking me questions. Her name was Fenya Bas (then Rosenfield), a Jewish girl from a nearby Shtundist village – the same Christian sect I had come across before, whose offer of shelter I declined because I refused to accept its religion.

"I was walking in the forest when suddenly I noticed a package far in the distance, lying under a tree," Fenya would tell me years later. "I approached it and discovered a little girl covered with a coat." Initially she got the impression I was no more than five years old, because of how shriveled and weak I had become. All the suffering I had been through, and the hardships of the past few days, had been burned into my face like a map. She spoke to me in Ukrainian and Yiddish, asking where my father was, what my name was and what I was doing all alone out there in the forest. I answered that Father had gone to look for food and never returned. She reached down to me, picked me up, and took me in under her coat.

In those moments, reality and dream were indistinguishable to me. I thought I was dreaming. I thought everything around me – the forest, Fenya's soft arms, her soothing voice – was happening in a dream. A beautiful angel had descended from the skies to embrace me in its arms to take me somewhere else.

And so, with me bundled up under her warm coat, she walked for quite some time until finally arriving at the home of another Shtundist back in the village. She told him I needed to be kept safe. I felt as though it was the angel of God speaking! Every syllable coming out of her mouth sounded like it had something divine to it, and I could see the Shtundist had great respect for her as well.

The Bas family, from right to left: David (fallen in the War of Independence), his girlfriend, Fenya Bas, and Ya'akov (Jacob) Bas. Italy, before the war.

Fenya Bass Tells the Story of how she Met Masha in the Forest:

"One day, as I am walking in the forest, I spot a package lying under a tree. I move closer and see that it's a girl… a girl, maybe five years old. That was Masha. She was half-frozen. I ask her: 'Who are you?' and she says: 'My name is Masha, and my father went to bring food. He didn't come back'. The Germans caught him. So I took her with me and she stayed with me until the end of the war."

Fenya Bas (née Rosenfield) tells the story to her grandchildren, excerpt of recorded conversation from: **Memorial book for the towns of Old Rafalowka, New Rafalowka, Olizarka, Zoludzk and vicinity**, p. 162, Tel Aviv, 1996

17 *The Shtundists*

Members of the Shtundist sect adhered religiously to the principle of indiscriminate love and acceptance of all human beings. It was a philosophy embedded deep within their soul. They believed that the act of protecting another from harm, which sometimes meant putting their own lives at risk, was a direct derivative of their faith, and that in doing so, they were fulfilling the will of God. They also believed that the Jewish people carried the word of God, and therefore protecting them in the dark times of the Holocaust was their sacred duty, and could lead them to transcendence.

They addressed each other as "brother" and "sister." They would often gather in the house that took me in and prayed together. Chanting in unison in a prayer of multiple languages, they looked as though the spirit of God rested upon them. "How can this be..." I thought to myself, making sure to remain as steadfast as I possibly could in my refusal to participate in their rituals. All of my thoughts and longing were now turned to Fenya. I yearned so much to see her again, to hear her voice, I yearned for her to come visit, even for a short time. She would occasionally come and go, each time making sure I was well, checking to see if the family was treating me as one of their own. And each time she left, her visit made me miss her intensely.

I would pass the time practicing various crafts. I learned how to knit and how to spin, peeled potatoes and helped in the kitchen. It was the beginning of 1944, and winter reigned fiercely outside. Looking out the window, I could see the shiny snowflakes coming down from the trees as they piled up on the ground covering everything in white. I thought about the forest, the partisan camp we had deserted in a panic, and the winter I had spent cooped up in the dugouts half-recessed into the ground.

But now I was safe in the hands of the Shtundists. I was in a neat and tidy home, with food on the table and a warm blanket to protect me from the harsh cold. The Shtundists treated me with dignity and respect. They wholeheartedly believed that I had been sent to their village by God so that I would survive. They regularly prayed with utmost devotion and sincerity, from the bottom of their hearts, and their faith gave me confidence. But the feeling of foreignness that had been with me everywhere I went wouldn't go away. I was a child taken in, and I knew I had to work for what I had received. I knew it was only thanks to Fenya and her special relationship with them that I was now safe and protected. I earnestly tried to satisfy them, to earn their trust, to diligently perform any task I was given, to be swift and efficient with my chores – all to win their affection, to get to hear a word of praise. I so badly wished they would tell Fenya good things about me. After all, despite my sincerest efforts, for the longest time I had been a burden on people; a child to be rid of.

The Shtundists

An evangelical sect founded in the latter half of the 19th century. The name "Shtundists" is derived from the German word "Stunde", meaning "hour", in reference to their practice of setting aside an hour every day for Bible study. Though originally used as a pejorative term by detractors of the group, over time it has been embraced by its members have embraced it as a legitimate moniker Shtundism has been influenced by German Baptistes, Pietists and Mennonites who settled in the southern regions of the Russian empire.

18 *The Typhus Epidemic*

It had become clear at that point that the Russian army was approaching, and that it was only a matter of time before the frontier expanded to include our village. Faint sounds of cannon fire could be heard from afar, further reinforcing the fact that they were getting closer and closer and that the balance of power had been tipped in our favor. These events rekindled the hope in people's hearts. The occasional airplane passed in the sky above us as well, and we knew liberation was imminent. People around me began to speak openly and confidently about the Germans being pushed back by the Russians. They were saying their prayers had been answered and that the war was coming to an end. Everyone was weak and in low spirits from years of hunger and poverty, from the exploitation of having their produce forcefully taken by the German army and its collaborators, from the heavy tolls of the occupation, the miserable living conditions, and the various epidemics and diseases that had broken out in the region.

The worst epidemic of all was typhus, and we all contracted it at one point or another. The Shtundist home I was staying at was located right behind the village cemetery, and whenever I'd climb up the bench near the window and look outside, I could see the funerals carried out there. A good portion of the villagers fell victim to disease. The house I lived in was not spared this fate, and one of the family members passed away. The typhus outbreak lasted several weeks, and I too fell ill with it. I had a very high fever, and most of the time I was either fuzzy or unconscious. Whenever I felt somewhat better, I'd climb the bench and watch what was happening outside. Seeing the funerals and all the people mourning, I said to myself, "Dear God, I have been through so much… And now I'm going to die here… And they're going to bury me here, in this desolate graveyard…" It wasn't death that scared me the most – I thought perhaps it would bring an end to my endless wandering, loneliness, and immense struggles to stay alive – but rather being buried in this gentile graveyard no one knew about… That was a terrifying thought.

But after a few weeks I recovered from the illness and soon regained my strength, prevailing yet again.

19 Liberation at Last

Near the end of winter in 1944, as the hills of snow began to melt and give way to the first signs of bloom and blossom, Fenya suddenly appeared, took my hand and said, "Come, Mashinka, I'm taking you to a territory where the war has already ended, a territory the Russians have freed and the Germans have retreated from."

I don't even know how I felt. We left the Shtundist village and started walking. We were free. We walked in broad daylight, in plain sight, passing through the backdrops of my childhood in Kamin-Kashyrskyi. The first town Fenya took me to was called Rafalivka.

We weren't the only ones: other Jews had also started arriving in Rafalivka. Jews who, like me, had managed to survive day by day, to stay alive in spite of all the death, loss, and adversity by hiding in the forests or in other places.

At the time, I had not yet realized that I was the only child from my hometown to survive. Suddenly I could be a child again. A Jewish child. I could walk the streets without anyone spitting at me, yelling out profanities, or trying to hurt me. The world had turned around to face the sun, and it was possible to live again.. However, the sadness resided deep within my soul. I now knew for certain I had neither a home nor a family to return to, and that everyone I loved, and everyone who loved me, was gone. The loneliness felt like a noose around my neck, constantly hurting, never letting up.

Unlike before, when I would allow myself to be lost in happy thoughts dreams about reuniting with my family after these dark times have passed, telling them all about what I'd been through and getting to hear them say how proud they are of me – I now knew there wasn't anyone to tell the stories to. And the immense pain from this realization sank in and was buried deep inside me.

I recalled Father had buried a certain amount of money in the ground at home and showed me the spot from which to dig it up. I knew I could get home and find the place with my eyes closed. After all, Father repeated the instructions over and over numerous times. Even so, I never did go back to get it, as Fenya and the others wouldn't let me go there by myself, and no one else in our group of survivors was from Kamin.

I longed for Aba Klurman and ached to see him again. He made sure to keep in contact with me. He knew where I was and promised he would come to Rafalivka as soon as he was released from the army. There was quite a large group of people in Rafalivka by then, and the place became a hub for Jewish survivors from all over the area. It wasn't long before a school was opened for the few children who have survived the war.

In my hometown of Kamin, only about a hundred Jews were left. Some survived by joining the partisan units in Ukraine and in White Russia[10], while others, like my maternal uncle Yaakov (Jacob) Plot, escaped to the homefront areas of the USSR. Only a minute number of people survived by staying in hideouts like I did. The 27th day of the Hebrew month of Av was declared The Kamin-Kashyrskyi Memorial and Mourning Day.

---

[10] From Wikipedia: "[White Russia is a historical term referring to] a territory in the eastern part of present-day Belarus."

20 *Rafalivka After the War*

I clung to Fenya as if she were my big sister. Before the war, she was engaged to a young man named Natan (Nathan) Bas, whose father was a pharmacist and owned a large pharmacy in Rafalivka. Natan and his mother were murdered, though his father survived in the forests, along with his son David and his daughter Rivka (Rebecca). He was a special man, generous and kind; in the days following the liberation, many Jews gathered around his pharmacy seeking to put a temporary roof over their heads. He took me in and even called me "daughter", though I never called him Father. For the first time in what seemed like an eternity, I felt like I wasn't alone, I felt I had a family. He would take me with him to the pharmacy, show me how different kinds of medicine were made, how to create compound powders for treating headaches and stomachaches, and promised me, like a proud father promising his daughter, that one day I will also become a pharmacist like him. I loved him very much, and I knew I was very dear to him.

He and Fenya, along with their other relatives, were my family. They looked after me, gave me strength, and showered me with attention and care. They took responsibility for me as if I were one of their own. Fenya continued to refer to me as her daughter, and I flourished by her side. Those were good moments in time, which allowed me to forget everything I'd been through, and those truly precious to me, if only for a short time.

The Bas household home a large and hospitable place. In addition to the Jewish survivors, several Russian-Jewish military officers gathered there as well. The war still raged on around us: military aircrafts constantly flew above our heads, and one Russian aircraft even crashed near us. Locomotives carrying soldiers and equipment passed us by on the nearby railway on their way to the frontier. The Germans kept dropping bombs and firing at the Russians, and it was not rare for us to be ordered to hide in the trenches to avoid the line of fire. Though the Russians implored us not to get careless or try to be heroes, and not to assume everything was already over, a strong sense of victory was in the air: here we are, alive, bearing witness to the Germans' defeat at the hand of the Russians. The Ukrainians will not hurt us again. It's okay to feel uplifted. Having been through all the terrible things we had been forced to endure, having survived the Germans and their collaborators – nothing could hurt us anymore. Whatever is going to happen next isn't important.

I was thirteen at this point, though I looked much younger. In Rafalivka I gradually returned to health and began taking care of myself, receiving treatment for medical issues which could not be addressed during the years of the war. Out of all of them, my teeth required the most urgent attention. They had become full of pus, which caused me constant, irksome pain. Over time I had learned to live with it, and during my time in the forest it became so regular that I had all forgotten about the existence of doctors, dentists, or any kind of a treatment for toothache. The pus constantly ran down from my mouth, and I would shove a piece of cloth in my mouth, wrapping it under my chin to cover the rotten teeth in my lower jaw. No one paid attention to things like that during the war, and no one would have been able to do anything about it anyway.

One day, we were visited by a Russian officer we knew as Captain Manov: a tall man with wide shoulders and a pleasant demeanor. He sat me down, looked into my eyes and asked me, "do you want to grow up and be tall?"

"Of course", I replied. "I want very much to be tall."

"Do you know what you've got there?" He asked, pointing at my mouth.

"No..." I answered, "I don't."

"You have a wound", he said. "A big wound, full of pus. It's not letting you grow, and it has to be treated. If you agree, I'll take you to a hospital where your wound will be treated, and then you will grow."

He was likely a trained doctor, and he made the arrangements for me to be flown in a military plane to a military hospital. Once there, I was admitted to the surgical department, as the hospital had no dental clinic. They had no means of anesthesia, either. One of the doctors or medics opened my mouth and four doctors armed with surgical knives cut the source of the infection and were eventually able to completely remove the infection. People who were standing outside the door at the time told me later that they crossed themselves because of how horrifying my screaming was. Even hours after the procedure had ended, I was still screaming in agony, begging them to give me something for the pain. But there was nothing to give; the war was still on and hospitals were likely out of medicine. It took days for the wound to heal, and it still required additional treatment afterwards.

In Rafalivka, everyone started talking about the future, about what had to be done going forward, now that the war was ending and there were no Jews left In Poland. Suddenly everyone wanted to go to the Land of Israel. It was clear to everyone that we had to leave the death-soaked soil of Poland, to get away from the bitter memories and the hateful environment. Some of the people in our group had already begun packing what little property they had left and move from the now-Russian controlled territory to the Polish side, to reunite with other groups of survivors. Zionism was now seen as the most pertinent and just cause to pursue. It would be a remedy for all the suffering and misery we'd been through, a source of hope for a new life in a new world – better world.

The Bas family stayed in Rafalivka for the time being, and their pharmacy was run under the protection of the Russians. When I was signed up to school, I requested to be registered as Masha Bas. In the days before the war, I was an honors student and received much praise. I tried hard to do well in school this time around as well, always listening to what the teachers said in class and studying diligently, but before long there was a change of plans; we packed what we could and relocated to the county town of Rivne, where there was already a strong Zionist presence in the form of activities organized by designated members of the Zionist movement, called "Schlihim" (Hebrew for "emissaries"), who had come from the Land of Israel to strengthen the connection of Jewish people in the diaspora to the Holy Land. The dream of making Aliyah was beginning to take shape and seemed more tangible than ever.

All the while, I kept waiting for my cousin Aba Klurman. I knew he was still fighting along with the rest of the partisans. Speakers all around town were broadcasting encouraging news about the German forces being pushed back by the ever-advancing Russian army, to the point of being forced into a hasty retreat to the west.

And then, one day, Aba Klurman finally showed. He had just recovered from typhus and was still getting his strength back. Having been recently dismissed from a military hospital, he looked pale and weak, and was barely able to stand, but I celebrated his arrival nonetheless. Knowing I had him there with me filled me with unimaginable joy. From that moment on, he became my legal guardian, as well as the one soul closest to me in the entire world. His family had a good amount of money and property left back in our hometown, and he was going back there to locate them. When it came time to say goodbye, I desperately begged him to take me along. "You're still little," he said, promising to return when he had enough money for the both of us.

21 | *I Arrive in Israel via Bucharest*

The Soviet authorities tried to impede the rise in organized Zionist activity, but it had already taken roots – even flourished – among the survivors, who would find clever and sophisticated ways to get around them unnoticed, and slip out of Ukraine and into the neighboring countries. Wherever there was a concentration of Jews, an extensive network of paper forgers was formed. People would pose as Polish, Greek or Italian foreigners, supposedly setting out for their home country, while in truth, their end goal was to arrive at the apotheosized Land of Israel.

As for our group, we got on a train to Poland and started our journey to Israel along with many other Jewish refugees. We exchanged names and identification papers and traveled south to the city of Lublin. Once there, we continued even further south, to the Poland-Romania border. We knew that this route would take us to the Black Sea, from which we'd be able to sail to the Mediterranean and then finally to the Haifa port in Israel. We had to stay under the Russians' radar and any encounters with them to the best of our ability, especially given their innately suspicious nature. Eventually we made it to Romania – more specifically, to Bucharest, the Romanian capital.

From right to left: Rivka Bas (first from the right), Masha (second from the right), and Yafa Bas (first from the left). Bucharest, 1945

The year was 1945. Post-war Bucharest saw many Jewish survivors from all over Europe gather at its gates, as it was a possible midway point which they could rendezvous and sail together to their new home of Israel. This led to a rise in Zionist activity in several locations throughout the capital:

Zionist pioneer youth movements, members of the Jewish Agency, Schlihim from the Land of Israel, and thousands of others came pouring in to the Mediterranean for the purpose of sailing to the Holy Land.

My cousin joined the Irgun, and had me join a group of children my age, put together with the help of the Agency and the Youth Aliya organization, in a local orphanage. The majority of the children were from Romania and other nearby countries. Each had their own story of survival through the war. Some had their entire families with them – parents, siblings, aunts and uncles – while others were orphans like me. Once again I felt different, like I didn't belong, like there wasn't a single soul I could lean on. I carved my own path, casting aside any difficulties and inconveniences. I tried to be pleasant and likeable, polite and agreeable, not wanting to lose what few relationships I managed to form with the others.

The orphanage was called the Maria Rosetti Home, and it was managed and maintained by the Joint, which also provided our every material need and prepared us for the Aliyah. Since the wound in my mouth was still open and had not yet fully healed, I was taken to the residential dentist. He gave me a friendly look and examined the wound. "You're going to the Land of Israel.

Doing laundry in the Beit Romano children's home, Bucharest, Romania, 1945. Masha is first from the right

Bucharest, Romania, 1945. First from the left– Masha. Second from the right – Hinda Likwornik, Sisel Klurman's sister. Third from the Right – Rivka Bas.

The Maria Rosetti Home, Bucharest, Romania, August 12, 1945. Masha is second from the right.

I didn't have any shoes of my own, so my cousin ordered a pair of comfortable new boots which I was very proud of. He gave an old Russian military shirt to a seamstress who sewed two pretty dresses out of it. He also paid a family from our hometown, who also awaited Aliyah, to look after me until we could see each other again in the Holy Land.

He himself managed to get an official immigration certificate with the help of his fellow Irgun members, who asked him to arrive early to assist them in their endeavors. He refused, however, opting to give the certificate to me and to Sisel (his girlfriend and future wife), who passed it on to her sister Hinde. These certificates were very expensive, and few were fortunate enough to have one. Most of the Jews who managed to get to Israel did not do so by going through the legal channels, but rather by arriving in illegal immigration ships without the permission of the authorities.

We departed from the Romanian port of Constanta aboard a ship named Transylvania in October 1945. Rivka Bas was on board, as well as other children I had been with at the orphanage. We all stood on deck, watching the continent of Europe slowly fade away into the distance. A few days later we reached our destination. At this sight of Mount Carmel towering above The Port of Haifa, my heart was flooded with a feeling of a dream come true.

The Irgun

While the war was still raging on in Europe, the Land of Israel was governed by the British as per the British Mandate, and several Zionist paramilitary organizations fought to drive them out of the Holy Land and establish an independent Jewish state on its grounds: the "Hagana" (Hebrew for "The Defense"), Lehee (an acronym of "Lohamei Herut Israel", lit. "Fighters for the Freedom of Israel", Hebrew: "לוחמי חירות ישראל") and "the Irgun" (Hebrew: האצ"ל, full title: Ha'Irgun HaTzva'ī HaLeūmī b-Ērētz Yiśrā'el, "הארגון הצבאי הלוחם בארץ ישראל", lit. "The Fighting Military Organization in the Land of Israel").

Szivélyes üdvözlet névnapjára!

A postcard given to me by Fenya
on the day we parted ways in Romania.
Kibbutz Uyara
6.18.1945

Blossom, blossom like a rose
Blossom, never wither
And when you reach our land do
not forget your duty
Work for your land
with all your might
And keep me in your heart inside

Your sister Fenya
For little Mashinka

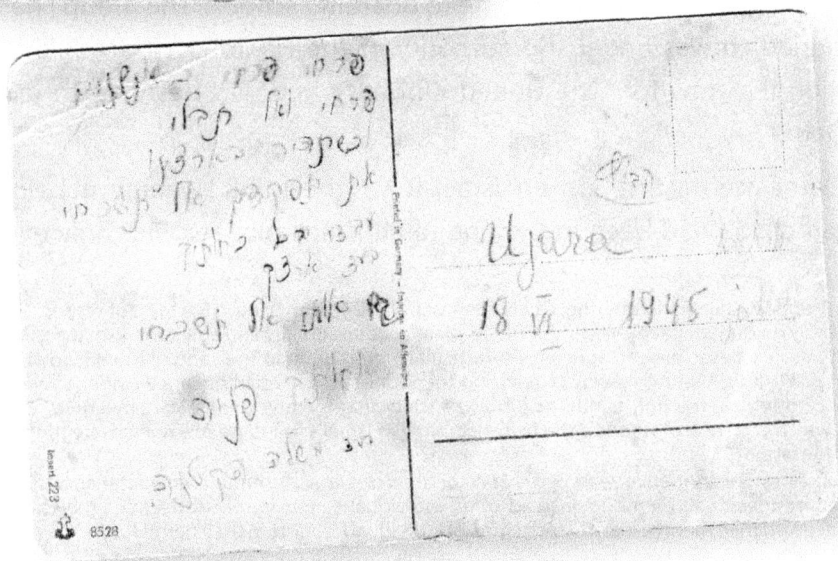

22 A New Land, a New Life

In the Land of Israel, a new chapter began. Blue skies, a golden sun, orchards and stretches of sand, Hebrew, the kibbutz[11]. There were so many new things we had to adapt to. A new society to assimilate into. We were in fact starting a whole new life, completely from scratch.

It was the month of November in 1945. Immediately after the ship docked at the Haifa port, our group was brought to a place called Ahuzat Yeladim (Hebrew for "Children's Mansion"). It was a magical-looking, inviting lodge at the heart of the lush Carmel forest. We were treated to a warm welcome by people who spoke kindly and graciously, and then shown to dining tables laden with all kinds of good food. I felt like we had walked through the gates of heaven.

As early as while we were still sailing, every child was assigned to one of four groups, each destined to be sent to a different destination based on internal considerations of the various supervising organizations. Some were sent to a kibbutz, some to a Moshav[12], and some to boarding schools. The group I had been assigned to was under the authority of the HaKibbutz HaMe'ukhad organization (Hebrew for "The United Kibbutz") and was destined to join Kibbutz Dafna.

Kibbutz Dafna was my first home in Israel. It was there that I went from being the orphan child I had been in Ukraine to an Israeli pioneer who only ever

---

[11] A kibbutz (Hebrew: קִבּוּץ, lit. "gathering, clustering"; plural: kibbutzim קִבּוּצִים) is a form of settlement almost entirely unique to Israel which implements ideas of communality and egalitarianism to form a community usually based around agriculture. Particularly prominent in The Land of Israel following the end of WWII, it was seen as a way of realizing the Zionist vision: building a new, independent, enlightened country in the Holy Land. The kibbutz society shares many ideological similarities with the USSR, which can be attributed to the fact that many of Israel's founding members were former citizens of the latter.

While kibbutzim in the formative years of the State of Israel had strict communal characteristics, such as an equal budget to all members instead of an individual salary, in recent decades they have gradually allowed their members a greater degree of individual freedom in their daily affairs.

[12] A moshav (Hebrew: מוֹשָׁב, plural מוֹשָׁבִים, moshavim, lit. settlement, village) is another form of settlement similar to a kibbutz. Though the two share similar ideologies, the moshav emphasizes values of individuality and is therefore less communal than the kibbutz.

speaks Hebrew, doing her best not to give away the truth about her tragic past. We were a group of about ten children between the ages of thirteen to fifteen, from various places around the world: Germany, Romania, and Poland. And though it was never explicitly stated, we were strongly encouraged to forget about everything. Focus on the present. Concentrate on starting anew. Forget, forget, forget.

We were even asked to change our names. But to me, the name Masha was my very identity, and I absolutely refused to change it. It was all I had left from my family, and I wasn't about to lose it too.

I was suggested the names Margalit and Miriam. Two of my female friends changed theirs to Aviva and Khaviva. I was so strongly pressured to change mine as well, that I almost gave in. But no… My name is Masha, I told myself. That was the name given to me by Father and Mother, and I will never change it to anything else.

As for the war and everything we'd been through, no one talked about any of it. It was clear to everyone that we don't talk about it, that we had to focus on the here and now, on the goals we had set out to achieve. The kibbutz picked a youth leader to guide us along, who served as our teacher and educator. He was very devoted to us, and truthfully wished to get closer to us and get to know us from the inside, understand our backgrounds and however little information we were willing to share about our pasts. And occasionally, in his fatherly way, he did manage to get us to trust and open up to him. Together with Khanna (Hannah) the housekeeper, he worked hard and made a genuine effort to help each and every one of us assimilate in the kibbutz and in society at large, to study and close the gaps we had in our education, to strike roots and heal from the deep wounds and scars of the war.

It was a prosperous time in terms of studying and education, but less so in terms of social life: some of the children in the group left Ahuzat Yeladim and went to live with their relatives in other areas across the country. I remember those moments whenever a relative of one of the children in our group arrived and told them, "We would like to adopt you. It's important that you get an education…" I would watch them from afar and my heart would break. I so badly wished I could be in that child's place.

While school and education were important in the kibbutz society, they were not the top priority. The leading values of all kibbutzim were the principles of communality, labor, and security. The best example of this was a Palmach training group who lived in Kibbutz Dafna, practicing a communal kibbutz lifestyle while also working the land and regularly interjecting security and protection activities into their routine. We all idolized the members of the group and identified with them. We desperately wanted to be like them. We saw them as a symbol of everything we wanted to be, the embodiment of what it meant to be a native to the Land of Israel... lively and liberated, tan-skinned and handsome, always with a confident expression on their faces. One of the members of said group was a young man by the name of Dudu (David), whose fall in the battle of Metzudat Koach inspired a famous Israeli song by the same name.

When we arrived at the kibbutz, we were treated to a warm welcome in the dining room. The entire crew was there to greet us with kind words and great enthusiasm. Everyone wanted to know what we had been through and how we survived.

In the beginning we didn't tell them anything. In fact, we didn't even speak about our pasts with each other. Each of us kept their life story and the

On horseback in Kibbutz Dafna, 1946

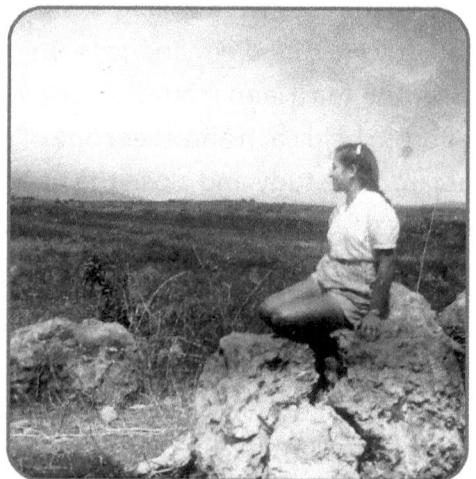

Masha in Kibbutz Dafna, 1946

circumstances of their survival to themselves. We didn't speak about the pain, about our orphancy, about how much we missed our loved ones, about all the suffering we'd endured, all the scars, all the death. We didn't bring up memories. All of that was kept locked away under a layer of thick skin, deep within the inner chambers of our soul.

It's likely we stood out somewhat in our appearance. Something about the look of Eastern European Jews, like what you'd see in photos of Jewish children from before the Holocaust. Whenever we heard songs in Yiddish, such as partisan anthems, tears would come to our eyes, but we did our best to cast those feelings aside and not dwell on our emotions, not give them away, not even think about them.

The kibbutz made a genuine effort to shower us with love, affection and warmth, to create a feeling of home, of safety and security, to make us feel like we belonged, and generally show us a path to a new life in a new direction. Over time, we gradually became accustomed to the kibbutz lifestyle and mentality. We connected to the cheerfulness of the native-born Israelis, learned the Hebrew language, the Hora dance and all the Hebrew songs, traveled the land and its scenery, and began to move away from the past and see the future taking shape.

Shavu'ot in Dafna, Masha is first from the right, 1946

Masha digging in Kibbutz Dafna, 1946

23 *Problems in Education...*

In May 1946, our teacher Mordechai Alter, published his thoughts and impressions as an educator working with our group, under the pseudonym Mordechai Ben Yitzhak. The article, titled "A Bundle of Letters", was featured in a magazine published by HaKibbutz HaMeuchad called "Alei Dafna" (Hebrew for "Leaves of Daphne"), and included his reflections, accounts, and dilemmas, all of which had to do with us. We somehow came across the magazine, worked out the names and quickly realized it was about us. I remember we were incredibly hurt. We felt our privacy had been severely compromised without our permission. We felt our inner selves had been exposed for the entirety of the kibbutz to see. The entire country, even. What hurt even more was the realization of how we were perceived, what others thought and said about us, and how much of a major issue our foreignness was, like a mark of Cain never to be washed away. It was an account Alter wrote in his journal in mid-November 1945. It's hard to fathom that it was written less than a year after we arrived in Israel from the inferno of the Holocaust.

The opening line was: "I was unable to expel the vileness and foulness that had stuck to them. In their hearts I have found but an empty space."

He went on to describe the difficulties he faced as a teacher dealing with our various unfavorable qualities: "Lies, disrespect for authority, exploitation – these are but the Imprints of the camps. A few of them also exhibit cruel tendencies, always out to get revenge, to hamper, to sabotage, to get forceful. Why not exploit the housekeeper to tidy up their rooms, just as they were exploited back in the camps..."

"Are they aware of the great debt they owe their own people whose blood was spilled to rescue them? Do they see our dedication and remain unappreciative? Sometimes their smile is but a cover for a scheme. When I look in their eyes, I see something distant and foreign... Distrust, fear, doubt."

He wrote about every single one of us. While he didn't mention us by name, we knew exactly which of us he was referring to.

About me he wrote: "Orphaned by her father and mother. Saved by a Christian woman from a village near her hometown, who harbored her in her home for a time. During the day she stayed in a pantry, and at nights she slept on a hearth." He added: "A girl hard as flint. her nickname within the group: "Di Partizanke (Yiddish for" little partisan girl"). Highly independent. Studies diligently."

The article was a hurtful, unforgivable slap in the face. We felt like we'd been thrown to the wolves once again. The whole ordeal made it abundantly clear to me that anyone who wasn't in the war could never possibly comprehend the scars it has left on us.

Our youth leader Avishai Ben Tzvi, who was a member of the Palmach training program, was genuinely interested in us, and genuinely wished we would open up to him and share our experiences from childhood and from the war with him. But everything was so complicated... We wanted to be like him, to feel like him, to become him, and put aside all the tragedy and pain. We wanted to be in the Palmach like him. To die for our country, even, and be the righteous heroes of a righteous war. To be unequivocally and indisputably Israeli. We instinctively picked up the notion that the more we managed to leave our past behind, the closer we came to becoming like the handsome, joyful, strong natives.

Masha "in the first days
of the Hebrew state", 1947

Upon joining the army when I was a few years older, I told myself with the pride of a young woman who had completed the transformation from a foreigner to a native Israeli, that no one knows I have no family, and no one would ever suspect that I was from "there..."

Our communal group in Kibbutz Dafna stayed together for about two years, up until 1947. We were about fourteen members, all in our adolescence. We had all but forgotten about our mother tongues and spoke exclusively in Hebrew. The hot sun had practically become a part of our identity, and we had completely adopted the kibbutz lifestyle and mentality. But one question always lingered as we looked out to the horizon: what next? We didn't want to stay in Dafna forever, and hoped to experience new things.

During that time, I even contemplated going to America. It turned out I had relatives who had been living there since before the war. I managed to find their address through the Search Bureau for Missing Relatives radio broadcast[13], and they even talked about the option of adopting me and giving me a home and a family with them in America.

I talked to Avishai about it, and he told me with a Zionist passion: "How dare you even think about something like that? You who have no roots here. Your entire family has been murdered. if you go to America, you'll be done with the Land of Israel for good. You can't go!"

I was very fond of him and his ever so-positive personality, and his words deeply affected me. I know today that there was nothing to prevent me from going and later coming back, and perhaps I shouldn't have heeded his advice. After all, there was nothing I needed more at the time than the love, support, and security which a family could provide.

Upon leaving Dafna, my journey of growth took me through various stations: Kibbutz Giv'at Haim where I studied and worked as part of a program by the

---

[13] The Search Bureau for Missing Relatives (or Relatives Search Department) was a department of the Jewish Agency formed in 1945 to assist survivors of the Holocaust in tracking down relatives and acquaintances who had gone missing during the war. To this end, a special radio program was created specifically to broadcast from Israel to the Jewish diaspora, which relayed names and requests from survivors hoping to reach out to their displaced relatives.

Youth Aliyah Zionist organization, Kibbutz Na'an where we formed a Gar'in[14] group for the purpose of founding a new, independent kibbutz, and in 1949, we joined a group of people who had made Aliyah like us in a place called Dardara, east of Lake Hula, in very close proximity to the Syrian border. We thought about becoming fishermen and making a living from fishing. The last station was Kibbutz Mishmar HaYarden, which we called "HaGovrim (meaning "The Prevailers" or "The Overcomers")" as a symbol for the personal journey each one of us had gone through. With every step I made along the way, I grew more and more eager to learn and evolve, expand my knowledge, and acquire an education. I was always heavily involved in all kinds of social and cultural undertakings.

Hakhshara[15] in Kibbutz Na'an, Masha is standing fourth from the right, 1948

---

[14] In the formative years of the State of Israel, the term Gar'in (Hebrew: גַּרְעִין, lit. kernel) was used to describe Zionist communal groups formed with the express purpose of consummating the Zionist vision of a Jewish revival in the Holy Land, mostly by founding and living in a new kibbutzim.

[15] From Wikipedia: The term "Hakhshara" (Hebrew: הַכְשָׁרָה), also Hakhsharah, Hachshara or Hakhsharah; lit. "preperation" or "training") is used to describe training programs (or the agricultural centers in which they are based) in Europe and around the world where Zionist youth learn technical skills that will assist them in their immigration to Israel and subsequent life in the kibbutzim.

In the newly founded kibbutz of Mishmar HaYarden, I requested to work in education as a school or kindergarten teacher. However, the general assembly voted, and I was ultimately assigned to kitchen duty.

I remember there was going to be a wedding in the kibbutz, and I was in charge of the baking and all other preparations. I thought for sure I'd be invited. When I found out I wasn't, I was deeply hurt. That was a true turning point for me. I didn't want to stay there any longer. So although I wasn't sure where I would go or what I would do, I announced I was leaving the kibbutz. I mustered up the courage to contact a relative by the name of Dora Barkai, who had previously told me that I would be welcome to stay with her if someday I decided to leave the kibbutz. I always remembered her words: "If you ever decide to leave the kibbutz, know that you have a home here."

I hitched a ride to Haifa where she lived and asked her up front if she remembered she had once offered me to come live with her, and whether the offer still stood. I was overjoyed to discover the offer was still relevant.

First days in Mishmar HaYarden, early 1950.
Masha is first from the left

She was the divorced single mother of a little girl named Rina, who was around six years old. She told me, "I will give you a home, and you will help me look after the girl..." And thus, we each fulfilled our part of the agreement with utmost commitment and dedication.

The real reason I left the kibbutz was my desire to serve in the army. At the time, there was an arrangement in place between the army and the kibbutzim watching the borders: any kibbutz member who chooses to watch over a border as part of their duty in the kibbutz will be considered as having served in the army, for all intents and purposes. But I remembered the time in the ghetto, and how badly Father and the others wished they could get their hands on weapons and fight back against the Germans, and ultimately decided in favor of joining the army.

I was considered one of the pillars of the young kibbutz, and had always had a central role in everything. People feared that my departure would open the floodgates for more to come. One of my male friends even said to me: "You'll come begging for us to take you back." And indeed, the next two years were tough, and I frequently found myself wishing I was still back there. But I was determined to study and achieve the goals I had set for myself, and so I enrolled in the teacher training seminar In Kibbutz Giv'at HaShlosha. Since I had no money to pay the tuition fee, I was forced to deal with residential and financial problems, all while carrying inside me a profound sense of loneliness, a burden made especially heavy during the holidays and every Sabbath. A year later, I graduated, received my kindergarten teacher diploma, and joined the Navy.

As early as when I was still in Kibbutz Dafna, I managed to track down relatives Father had mentioned, who had come to Israel before the Holocaust, and get in touch with them. We regularly keep in touch to this day. In the years that followed, I found several other relatives of mine who were also in the Holocaust.

A flat tire on a trip to Eilat with the Navy quartermasters 'division, 1953. Masha is sitting at the top

Masha with her preschool students, Bethlehem of Galilee, 1953

Student card, Giv'at HaShlosha seminar, 1951

Everything Dormant and Forgotten is Awakened by Love

I met Yehezkel after my discharge from the Navy, on a trip along the Kinneret.

The most important thing for me back than was to meet someone who had not been in the Holocaust. I couldn't explain it, but my instinct told me I needed someone who didn't know the pain of loneliness, who wasn't carrying any scars; someone free from bitter memories, with a normal life and a home that would feel natural to return to, with a family of parents and siblings and joyful get-togethers. My eternal longing for my grandmother whose embrace I so terribly missed made me swear that when I have children of my own, they would have a grandpa and grandma! I developed a sophisticated inner radar that could instantly detect who was a Holocaust survivor carrying pain like me, and just steered clear of them.

Yehezkel arrived in Israel with his parents Max and Tzila and his sister Rakhel (Rachel) in 1935. When the Nazis rose to power, Max and Tzila foresaw the looming danger, left everything behind and made haste for Israel, upon which they settled in Haifa. Their relatives who stayed in Europe all perished In the Holocaust, but here, in this young society in a new land, even as few as four people could be considered a whole family.

In the year 1943, at the age of fourteen, Yehezkel joined the Irgun. His first commander was Yitzhak (Isaac) Buzaglo, whose alias within the organization was Avinoam (Hebrew: אבינועם). Buzaglo was wounded when a makeshift grenade went off in his pocket while he was protecting his squad on a mission to hang posters around the city.

Upon graduating the Irgun Squad commanders' course, Yehezkel was given the alias "Arnon." This alias would later be changed to "Eyal" upon his graduation from the Irgun's platoon commander course, celebrated in a ceremony at Fort Shuni, near Binyamina, on Hanukkah of the same year.

Yehezkel in military uniform,
1948

Yehezkel, 1948

During his time in the Irgun, Yehezkel held various positions: he was in command of three squads in the organization's publicity corps (Hebrew: חת"מ, acronym for "חֵיל תַּעֲמוּלָה מַהְפְּכָנִי", lit. Revolutionary Publicity Corps), served in the armory at Camp Vardia, and for a while, was in charge of transporting packages to the Irgun base in Safed.

In early 1948, Yehezkel made his way to a mission in Fort Shuni. The plan was for him to pose as a British soldier and, along with other Irgun members in three different vehicles, infiltrate a British military base near the village of Tira, on the outskirts of Haifa, and use forged papers to gain access to firearms which would then be secretly delivered to the Irgun. In the middle of the operation, however, he was wounded by gunfire coming from the Arab village of Ayn Ghazal, near Zikhron Ya'akov. A medic named Margalit was with him when it happened and tended to his wounds until they arrived at the Palmach base in Kibbutz Maayan Tzvi. From there, he was transferred to Hadassah Hospital in Tel-Aviv.

During the operation to capture Wadi Nisnas in Haifa, Yehezkel was in charge of operating the Irgun's two Bren machine guns. He commanded over the entire neighborhood for a whole 24 hours, working in coordination with Hagana forces to clear the perimeter.

After he joined battalion 57 of the newly formed Israeli Defense Force (IDF) which comprised former Irgun members, he went into Camp Tzrifin armed with an Sten submachine gun and fought off Egyptian aircrafts as a duty officer.

In the spring of 1948, as the events of the Altalena affair[16] unfolded off the shores of Tel-Aviv, Yehezkel was at the IDF Tel Nof airbase, on a machine gun operator training course. Upon graduating, he joined the 13th battalion's special reconnaissance unit, under the leadership of Avraham (Abraham) Yafe. The plan was for the unit to gather near Beit Netofa Valley and mount an assault against Fawzi al-Qawuqji, a leading figure in the Arab Liberation Army, but it was ultimately abandoned, and the operation never came into fruition.

When Yehezkel fought in the Battle of 'Auja El Hafir' on the southern front, his left arm was hit by shrapnel from a blast, thus bringing his role in the War of Independence to a close. Dov Shapira and Yehuda Cohen, who were close friends of Yehezkel's since their time serving together in the Irgun, were both killed on impact. Yehezkel was evacuated in a jeep to a battalion aid station, from which he was transported to a military hospital in an ambulance towed by a tractor. Once he recovered, he was assimilated into the Navy.

---

[16] The Altalena Affair was a violent confrontation between the newly formed IDF and the Irgun in June 1948. The confrontation broke out when an Irgun cargo ship named Altalena arrived at the coast of Tel-Aviv, loaded with firearms purchased beforehand to assist in the struggle to drive the British out of the Land of Israel. Due to unexpected delays, the ship arrived several weeks later than planned, at a time when a truce was in effect between the British and the IDF. Knowing that bringing in illegally purchased firearms into the country would break the uneasy truce, the IDF demanded that the Irgun surrender its weapons. When the latter refused, the army responded by shooting down the ship and sinking it along with the people onboard.

21.6.56

21.6.56

To the dearest woman in the world entire,

I have just returned home from my journey to see your majestic gleam, and as I was making the long way back, my mind and thoughts revolved around nothing but you. You—Masha.

I thank you for everything: for your warm reception and for your joy upon seeing me. It flatters me greatly indeed.

I rather hastily departed your residence, as I had been contemplating the question of how not to have my heart torn when I leave, and it escaped me that I had no certain way of knowing whether or not you will travel to Tel-Aviv. If you decide that you shall, and if this decision comes to you on the evening of Friday, call me around 6:30-7:00 PM at my address of Arlozorov St. 128. You will find the name in the phonebook. Save yourself the trouble of calling YIsrael.

It is possible I may not arrive on time. Do not worry, I said I would come, and come I shall—even if only by the afternoon.

If you would be so inclined, discard the withered flowers in the vase. Keeping them is uncomely, and it is as though they gaze frowningly upon me for not bringing you a fresh bouquet in their stead. So very beautiful are you, my dear, and so beautiful is your hair swept upwards, endowing your neck with an aura of noble grace.

With utmost love,

get well soon,

Yehezkel

English translation of the letter on the previous page

25 *Our Life Together*

Masha and Yehezkel's Wedding Day, July 25, 1956

On the 25th of July 1956, Yehezkel and I took each other for husband and wife, and so began the era of joy in my life. It felt like from that moment on, there would be only the good and the serene, and we could finally focus on working, evolving, and raising a family.

But the biggest joy of all was yet to come: about a year later, in September 1957, our eldest son Yaron was born, and in March 1963 came our daughter Limor, and I felt like I was the luckiest person on Earth.

During this period of a few years, I stopped working as a kindergarten teacher and dedicated myself entirely to motherhood. I loved being a mother, and I take pleasure in reminiscing about my children's days of babyhood: the first smile, the first step, the first word… I loved diapering them, feeding them, playing with them, watching them grow and develop from children into mature adults and, before I could notice, into two fine, awe-inspiring people.

We purchased an apartment on 83 Hanita Street, where I still reside to this day. We were always content with our lot; our livelihood needs were quite minimal back then, and it didn't take much to make us happy. It was a time when everyone lived modestly, and what we had was entirely sufficient. We felt as though the future ahead was entirely within our grasp, and aspired to succeed and get to a point where we could be financially independent. We were young and hard-working, and every moment in the home we built together, in the life we built together, was filled to the brim with love and joy.

Up until the birth of Yaron, I worked as a kindergarten teacher in Migdal HaEmek under the Working Mothers Association. Upon his birth I took a leave of absence which lasted several years, and only went back to work when the children were a little older. I worked as a kindergarten teacher for about twenty-five more years after that. I loved my profession, loved the children, and had excellent relationships with their parents. I felt I had been blessed for having everything always run smoothly, for having had the fortune to enjoy what I did for a living, for having found my place in the community and be a part of the educational system in the State of Israel, and for being able to celebrate holidays in Hebrew, singing songs and telling stories, all while seeing Israel gradually build and evolve, becoming the home of many wonderful, gifted children.

My children grew and became adults, each acquiring an education: Yaron married his wife Karin, graduated from the Technion-Israel Institute of Technology with a Ph.D. in computer science, and works at IBM as the lead manager of various projects. My daughter Limor took up architecture, also at The Technion, and runs an independent firm together with her husband Ron. Yaron and Limor each have three children of their own, and we have all shared a great many joys and family get-togethers.

With Yaron and Yehezkel, 1959

With Limor and Yaron, 1963

26 Today, the Past is a Part of Me

During the time of my military service, The Diary of Anne Frank was first published, garnering much attention from the public and evoking reactions of sympathy and outrage at every turn. The thunderous silence around the events of the Holocaust was suddenly beginning to crack. Everyone was talking about Anne Frank. I remember sitting in my room at the base and reading The Diary, thinking about all the noise it stirred up and listening to conversations my friends were having about it, to their emotional reactions to the terrible suffering the Jews in Europe had to endure, as reflected in her story.

In me, however, her story evoked a very different feeling. Why is everyone so worked up over the story of Anne Frank, I thought… Unlike what I had been through, she had friends and her sister and her parents together with her in her hideout as she was writing her story. Indeed, everything she went through did not even amount to a tiny fragment of what I went through. Unlike her, I was on my own for almost three years, going through unspeakable hardships without a single close soul to lean on. To this day, I hear myself repeat time and again in my heart: it cannot be explained, it cannot be understood. Words simply cannot describe it.

To this day I am deeply distraught, outraged, by the notion that that the Jews in the Holocaust "went like lambs to the slaughter." Over the years I would always bite my tongue and hold myself from speaking up whenever I heard this claim, wanting to scream in protest at this wrongful statement. But I never did speak up, never did scream. And when I cried, it was with no tears, and only in the depths of my heart.

How could one explain the strong urge to carry on living when everyone you have ever loved, and who has ever loved you, has been murdered…

How could one explain what a ten-year-old girl feels as she is chased by murderous Ukrainians out to kill her, and not only her, but every living Jew, from infants to adults to elderly.

121

How could one describe surviving in the freezing Ukrainian forests, the repeated raids, the dead bodies in the snow, the alienation that spread among the people, and the desperate attempt to cling to life in spite of it all…

How could one explain any of those things…

In 1972, I heard the radio reports about the massacre of the Israeli athletes at the Munich Olympics. I remember the utter shock and the shivers I felt going down my spine. The past, dormant within my soul, resurfaced and overwhelmed me once again. I again saw the images of foreign, hostile villages in my mind's eye. What struck me the most in those moments was… There they were in Munich, with the entire world watching, in the age of television… All the precautions and security measures taken ultimately couldn't prevent the terrible massacre – and yet, no one in their right mind imagined saying those athletes went like lambs to the slaughter.

The millions who perished in the Holocaust, however, will forever be stained by this notion. I wish very much I could forgive, and yet I can't. In my younger years, whether it was during my time in the Kibbutz, in the army, or when I lived in the city, I always felt a sort of shame telling people I was a Holocaust survivor. There was just something about the way people looked at me whenever I told them I was born in Poland. It felt as though I carried the mark of Cain on my forehead, never to be lifted. Why?

As the years went by, a newfound sense of pride awakened in me. Pride about the fact that I survived, about the immense strength with which I stood in the face of adversity, about having managed to stay alive by my own courage, dexterity, and sheer force of will, while so many others, braver, bolder and more gifted than me, could not.

I find myself going over the elaborate survival plan Father planned out for me again and again in my head: the escape from the ghetto, the jacket full of family photos, the path he laid out for me, his detailed instructions. Father meticulously planned every last detail, drawing maps and doing everything he could to ensure I survived. Not a lamb led to the slaughter, but the exact opposite: Father was preparing me on that day, to grow up, to mature, to stay alive.

There was a time when I repressed this chapter of my life story, locking it away in the hidden depths of my mind. When a memoir about the community of Kamin-Kashyrskyi was published, I was happy to be among its contributors, submitting a short segment in the memory of my community and my loved ones.

My daughter Limor was in 6th grade at the time, and schools in the young State of Israel had just begun teaching students about the Holocaust. One day, she came home and said all students had been asked if anyone had Holocaust survivors in their family who could come to class to tell their story. She told her teacher that her mother was "from there", and about the segment I had submitted to the memoir. It was important to her to bring it to class and read it to her classmates. I agreed right away, but something inside of me trembled. Maybe I was afraid of bringing out my true identity which I'd kept hidden away for many years.

"Limor honey", I said, "take the book, but promise me that if you feel the students don't want to listen, you will stop immediately."

The following day, I couldn't stop thinking about her. I was waiting for her to come home to tell me how it was and if everything went smoothly.

"Mom," she said as soon as she came through the door, "Mom, the whole class was sitting with their mouths open, no one made a sound, and the teacher asked me to continue reading the story to the class on Friday!

This was such a wonderful and emotional moment for me. Something was finally lifted off me. So many years of silence, of repression, of sweeping things under the rug, finally came to an end. I suddenly learned that people did want to listen. They did want to know. That they did want me to tell.

With time, the anger and pain towards Father that had been stirring inside me also gave way to forgiveness and reason. Though my longing and immense love for him never waned as the years went by, I also couldn't help but be angry with him for abandoning me that day in the forest. I could never bring myself to put aside the anger and be grateful to him for being the person without whom I would never have survived. Those feelings were emotionally charged and condensed; I missed him immeasurably, while at the same time I felt a scathing, tormenting resentfulness towards him. Father who loved me, who used to tell me stories about the family… Father who had left me to live without him in the forest.

Only when my eldest son was born did this bitter anger begin to subside. His birth showed me that there was no greater love than a parent's love for their child. For the first time ever, I was able to identify with Father and see what immense mental strength he had to muster to leave me in the forest, with all that information he did his best to embed into me, which I still hold in my memory to this day. The inner alliance between him and me was now that much stronger.

In one of my meetings with Fenya Bas, I told her about that moment when all my anger just faded away. She said to me, "Mashka, you've never told me this before… You said your father went to look for food and never returned…"

When my son Yaron graduated high school, I arrived at his graduation ceremony proud and excited. I felt as though all my hopes and dreams had become a reality and the universe was showering me with good fortune. Here I am in The Land of Israel, with my wonderful family, and my two amazing children are devoted, gifted students. There isn't a mother in the entire world prouder than I am. I dressed up in festive clothes and left the house arm in arm with Yehezkel.

But something unexpected happened on stage which shattered my euphoria. The students, eighteen years-old youths soon to be recruited into the IDF, put up a play they had written and directed based on their trip to the Saint Catherine Monastery in Sinai Peninsula.

One of them got up on stage and crossed himself… And suddenly I was flooded by a stream of memories, associations, and emotions threatening to drown me. I was once again there, in the time of the war, a little girl arguing with a man who seeks to save me, refusing to commit heresy by making the sign of the cross. That girl would rather die than perform that gesture and betray her own Judaism.

My entire body responded to that one short gesture on stage. My skin crawled and my vision became blurry. In that heart-wrenchingly painful moment, I realized that the war still had a very strong effect on me, clutching at my throat, leaving me helpless to resist its influence.

It's a shame I've kept quiet all these years, I told myself… It's a shame I never gave those memories a proper expression. It's a shame I've never talked about how important it was to me to stay Jewish.

As the years passed, I learned to speak openly about it and let my voice be heard. I no longer bother myself with questions such as whether it's right, whether people will believe me or not, or whether I will find the words to properly convey the true depth of the darkness that had descended upon the world.

I go wherever people will listen. I never refuse an invitation. I am loyal to my inner urge to talk about the past, doing my best to describe the events in detail in the hope that what I felt gets carried over through my words.

And whenever that happens… The lines between past and present all but disappear. Images long forgotten once again resurface and appear before me… Things just come to me… Like the names of people I'm not even sure how I know…. Moments from an eternity ago suddenly come back, just like that.

27 *My Cousin Aba Klurman*

My cousin Aba's family, the Klurman family, was a big, established family in our town. Aba was the oldest of Menucha Plot and David Klurman's seven children.

When the occupation began, he was among the first to run off into the forests and join the partisans. He escaped the ghetto along with a group of friends in the summer of 1942 and joined an independent group of Jewish partisans. In time, they were joined by other Jews, and the group eventually joined up with the Soviet partisan unit led by Kruk. During his time as a partisan, Aba Klurman participated in many combat missions: sabotaging railways, rigging trains to explode, destroying bridges, mounting assaults on police stations and more. For his excellent performance in these operations he received the Order of the Red Banner and "Medal for Victory" decorations from the Soviet army.

Before the ghetto was terminated, Aba Klurman and his father David agreed that if worst came to worst, the family would flee to the nearby village of Dovzhyk, where they would find temporary shelter with a gentile friend, a farmer by the name of Ivan, who would take them to a safe haven at the heart of the forest. Immediately after the ghetto's final termination, Aba Klurman made it to the farmer's residence, where he was informed that his family had been murdered by the Ukrainian militia the day before. Ivan the farmer pointed to a dirt mound in his yard and claimed that was the burial site of his family – his parents, his ten-year old sister, and his two brothers aged five and nine – along with my own mother and Moisha'le, my seven-year-old brother. Until the day he died, Aba Klurman remained suspicious that it was Ivan who murdered his family.

In 1944, Aba Klurman fell ill with typhus, lost consciousness and was taken to a military hospital. After he recovered, he said his mother had come to him in a dream and said to him… "As if our death wasn't enough, why do the horses and their carriages have to pass through our graves?!" Aba rushed to the village of Dovzhyk. There he met Ivan's wife, who led him to a dirt mound different than the one Ivan had pointed to. Indeed. This was a country road which many horse-drawn carriages passed through every day. Aba marked the spot with a pole planted firmly in the ground in the hope of one day going back there.

After the end of the war, Aba joined the Bricha movement[17] in Europe. He was among its founding members. Together with Avraham Lidovski, he set out from Rivne to Chernivtsi to examine the possibility of passing through the Romanian border. There he met Sisel, his future wife. The two of them set out for Italy, where Aba brought together a group of Beitar movement activists, and they established a branch which would handle all kinds of affairs related to the Bricha movement, with their home in Rome serving as the central gathering place for its members. It was there that their eldest daughter Tzipora was born.

When an emissary of the Irgun arrived in Italy, Aba joined the efforts to end the British Mandate in Israel from afar. When the concentration of Jewish refugees in Italy began to diminish as a result of many of them immigrating to Israel, Aba and Sisel moved their operations to Romania, where they both worked to lay the foundations of local Irgun cells.

Following the establishment of the State of Israel, Aba, Sisel and their little daughter made Aliyah and came to the Holy land. After struggling for some time with the hardships of living in the young country, however, they opted to try their luck in the United States. They managed to establish and maintain expansive business ventures over there, and yet never abandoned the dream to settle down in Israel. Years later, they finally fulfilled their wishes and came to Israel to live in Ramat Gan. They lived there until Aba's health made the constant flying difficult to bear, at which point they returned to the United States.

With the Perestroika policy in effect in the USSR of the Nineties, it was finally possible to travel back to Ukraine to locate the burial sites of our deceased

---

[17] [From the official website of the Bricha Legacy Association:] "The 'Bricha' movement operated in Europe from the end of World War II until the establishment of the State of Israel, and was responsible for the smuggling of some three hundred thousand Holocaust survivors from Eastern Europe to the southwest, to the ports of the Mediterranean – survivors who chose to abandon the killing valley of Europe in order to establish a home for themselves in the Land of Israel."

family members and townsfolk. Aba, along with his wife Sisel, the late Avraham Bieber, the late Archik, his wife and myself traveled to Kamin-Kashyrskyi and its neighboring village of Dovzhyk. This was in August 1990.

The village of Dovzhyk no longer existed, and none of the locals recalled a village by that name ever being there. Aba Klurman attempted to find older locals who lived in the time of the war and were still alive then. Fortunately, we found two elderly women, one of whom said she used to work as a housemaid in the Klurman household. She hurriedly called in an old farmer living nearby, and he confirmed he had lived in Dovzhyk until the day it was destroyed by order of the government at the time when the area was under Soviet rule. The elder remembered the farmer named Ivan and said he could bring us to the spot where his house had formerly stood. He also vividly remembered that this was the spot where a family of seven had been murdered during the war. We got him in the vehicle and started to drive. Along the way, we were also joined by the mayor of Kamin, and together we started driving through the forest, with him directing us. The ride went on for hours. I had a feeling we were driving in circles. It didn't make sense for it to be so long, given that the village was supposed to be much closer, and the forest surrounding us was too young. Aba Klurman pointed this out as well.

Just when I was beginning to lose hope that we would find what we'd come for, we stopped the car and the old farmer started walking around the woods. Then he suddenly stopped, smelled the air, pointed at a small dirt mound about 15 cm wide, and said: Right here! They were buried right here! He began describing everything as if it was happening right then and there! He described how three people had been there: three adults – one male and two females – and four children. He described how many boys and how many girls there were, what they wore, and how they tried to flee, ran, and got shot.

We all stood there dumbstruck!

Aided by a local school principal – an ex-partisan who Aba Klurman had known from the war – and thanks in no small part to the dollars that the Aba magnanimously handed out, we managed to get all the necessary permits to dig up the grave. In the pit we found seven skeletons, just like we'd suspected.

They were the bones of Aba Klurman's parents David and Menucha, his sister Masha, and his two brothers Yehoshua (Joshua) and Tzvi, as well as my mother Freidel and my dear brother Moisha'le. On the same spot, we also found a piece of the pole Aba had marked the site with back in the year 1944. We collected all the remains into a crate and transferred them to the Jewish mass grave at the town graveyard.

In May of 1991, Sisel and Aba Klurman went back to Kamin to retrieve the remains of their loved ones and bring them to Israel for reburial. On May 21, 1991, in an exemplary ceremony attended by family, friends, acquaintances, and Kamin survivors, their remains were brought to eternal rest in the Qiryat Shaool cemetery. Rabbi Israel Lao, then the Chief Rabbi of Tel-Aviv Jaffa, and the Speaker of the Knesset at the time, Mr. Dov Shilansky, were among the attendees. The gravestone placed over their grave about six months later was designed by my daughter Limor, granddaughter of my mother. It was dedicated not only to our relatives, but also to the memory of all the Holocaust victims from Kamin and the surrounding area, as well as the Jewish fighters who fell in Kamin fighting against the Nazis and their associates.

After fifty years, Aba Klurman could finally say Kaddish for the members of his family and mourn them in accordance with the Jewish law.

The search in the forest

ב"ה

ונקיתי, דמם לא נקיתי

הרינו להודיע לקרובינו, ידידינו, מכרינו ובני עירנו והסביבה שלאחר מאמצים מרובים, זכינו לגלות את מקום רציחתם ולהעלות
ארצה את ארונותיהם של קרושינו ויקירינו:

דוד בן למל הכהן **קלורמן**   **פריידל** בת משה (לבית פלוט) **דרייצין**

מנוחה בת משה (לבית פלוט) **קלורמן**   **משה** בן זלי"ג **דרייצין**

מאשה בת דוד הכהן **קלורמן**

יהושע בן דוד הכהן **קלורמן**

צבי בן דוד הכהן **קלורמן**

שנרצחו ע"י הנאצים ועוזריהם בנובמבר 1942 – מר חשון תש"ג ליד הכפר דוביצק שליד קמין קושירסקי פלך והלין.
סדר הבאתם למנוחת עולמים יתקיים ביום שלישי, ח' סיון תשנ"א, 21 למאי 1991 בשעה 4.00 אחה"צ בבית העלמין קרית שאול ת"א.

שמואל אבא וזיסל קלורמן   יחזקאל ומאשה (לבית דרייצין) וולפסטאל   ובני ביתם

אוטובוס יעמוד לרשות הקהל ליד קופת היכל התרבות ת"א, רח' הוברמן, בשעה 3.15 אחה"צ.

For I will cleanse their blood, which I have not yet cleansed

We hereby inform our relatives, friends, acquaintances, townsfolk, and district that after much effort, we managed to uncover the murder site of our cherished loved ones, who were killed by the Nazis and their associates in November 1942 in the village of Dovzhyk, close to the town of Kamin-Kashyrskyi of the Volyn Oblast.

They will be brought to their final resting place in a reburial ceremony on Tuesday, May 11th, 1991 at 6 PM at the Qiryat Shaool cemetery in Tel-Aviv. A bus will be available for the public near the ticket office of Heichal Hatarbut Tel Aviv. Huberman St. at 3:15 PM

The bulletin announcing the reburial ceremony of the Klurman and Dreitzen families.

במבצע בלשי איתר הבן את עצמות בני משפחתו שנרצחו בשואה והביאן לקבורה בארץ

47 שנים לאחר שנספו בשואה הוריו, שלושת אחיו הקטנים, דודתו ובנה, הצליח איש-עסקים יהודי מארה"ב, שמואל אבא קלורמן, למצוא את הקבר בעיירה הרוסית הנידחת □ כל השנים זכר את חלומו בו הופיעה אמו ואמרה לו: "לא די שנהרגנו, אלא ששוסים ועגלות עוברים על הקבר שלנו"

— מאת שלמה נקדימון, כתב "ידיעות אחרונות"

איש-עסקים יהודי מארה"ב, שמואל אבא קלורמן, הצ־ ליח לזהות בעיירה הרוסית הנידחת את מקומות עצמותיהם של שבעה מבני משפחתו, שנרצחו בשואה. העצמות הובאו ארצה בסוף השבוע, ותו ייטמנו מחר בקבר אחים בבית-העלמין בקריית-שאול.

משפחת קלורמן התגוררה בעיירה קמי׳ניקאשירסקי שבמ־ חוז והלין. במקום התגוררו כ-3,000 יהודים, שרובם הוצאו להורג בשלוש אקציות. אבא קלורמן, אבא קלורמן עם אביו, דוד קלורמן, יצאו לפרטיזנים, סיכם עוד קודם כדי עם אביו, דוד קלורמן, הצטרפו לשורות הפרטיזנים, ואף חייל של הצבא ומשפחתו שהתאספו להסמיד את היהודי הגיש למקום, הם ימלטו לכפר וסמוך דוביצק, שם הוצאו מסתתר אצל גוי פולני בשם איוון, שהיה ידיד המשפחה.

שיבעה מבני המשפחה אבן הגיע למקום, אך שעות ספו־ רות לאחר מכן נרצחו. איך וכיצד? האם הגוי איוון בגד למקום הקבר. היה זה במקום שונה מזה, שממאתאי היו קבורים בני משפחתו, אבל אשתו של איוון הצביע עליו בזמנו. על גללית הקרקע, שממאתאי היו קבורים בני משפחתו, אבן עברו סוסים ועגלות. אבא קלורמן תקע יתד במקום. תיכנן לחזור לקבר לאחר...

פגישה עם אחים לנשק

זמן-מה לאחר מכן חלה אבא קלורמן ואושפז בבית-חו־ לים בכפר מקומי. "לפתע", מספר קלורמן, "אמו נגלתה אלי בחלום. היא אמרה לי את הדברים הבאים: 'לא די שנהרגנו, אלא ששוסים ועגלות עוברים על הקבר שלנו'. קלורמן חרס אז את הדברים בזיכרונו. לאחר שהשתחרר מבית-החולים יצא שוב לכפר דוביצק, לביתו של איוון. הוא לא מצא אותו, אבל אשתו של איוון הובילה אותו למקום הקבר...

אבא קלורמן (צילום: שאול גולן)

הארגז ובו הגולגלות ועצמות בני המשפחה, לאחר שאותרו בדוביצק

In Detective Endeavor, Son Locates Remains of Relatives Murdered in the Holocaust, Brings Them to Israel for Reburial

47 years after his parents, three little brothers, aunt and cousin perished in the Holocaust, Jewish-American businessman Samuel Aba Klurman successfully located their burial site to a backwoods Russian town. In all those years, he never forgot the dream where his mother appeared to him and told him: "As if being killed was not enough, now horses and carriages are passing through our grave."

- Written by Shlomo Nakdimon, reporter for Yediot Aharonot -

Jewish-American businessman Samuel Aba Klurman has successfully identified a mass grave where the remains of seven of his family members who were murdered in the Holocaust had been buried. The remains were flown to Israel over the weekend and will be reburied tomorrow in a communal grave in the Qiryat Shaool cemetery.

The Klurman family lived in a community of about 3,000 Jews in a town named Kamin-Kashyrskyi in the Volyn region in Poland, the majority of whom were executed over the course of three Aktions. Just before he joined the partisans, Aba Klurman made an agreement with his father David: when his family members sensed that termination of the ghetto was imminent, they would flee to the nearby village of Dovzhyk, where they would find shelter with Ivan, a Polish goy who had been on friendly terms with the family. The seven of them acted accordingly when the time came and made their way to Dovzhyk, but were murdered but were murdered a mere few hours later. How and why? Did the goy, Ivan, betray? Aba Klurman does not have the answers to these questions. He had been keeping contact with the people of Dovzhyk, and upon learning that his family members had reached the place, he hurriedly got there as well. Though he arrived just a single day after them, they were no longer alive.

All Ivan told him was: "A Ukrainian militia man serving the Germans executed the members of the family." He also pointed to the spot where they had been buried. He said The Ukrainian militia man had shot them dead.

Aba Klurman had no way of verifying Ivan's story, or any other details about the circumstances of the death of his family. To this day, he is gnawed by doubts about the truthfulness of this story told by the "friend", and by the possibility that it was him who turned them over.

A Meeting with Brothers in Arms

Sometime later, Aba Klurman fell ill, and was admitted to the local hospital. "Suddenly", he recounts, "my mother appeared to me in my dream, and said the following: Not only were we killed, but horses and carriages pass through our graves." Klurman etched these words into his memory. After he was released from the hospital, he went back to Dovzhyk, to Ivan's house. Though he did not find Ivan, the farmer's wife led him to the spot where the grave was. It was a different dirt mound than the one Ivan had pointed to before, but horses and carriages had indeed been regularly passing through this one, underneath which his family members were buried. Aba Klurman marked the spot with a pole, as he had plans to go back there after the war and wanted to have some sort of sign to find it when he did.

Klurman would continue to fight under the partisans and would later join the ranks of the Bricha movement and the European cell of the Irgun. During his time in the Irgun, he participated in various operations, including the bombing of the British embassy in Rome. He lived in Israel for a while before settling down in the United States, where he waited for the opportunity to return to Russia and redeem the remains of his family members. It wasn't until the era of the Perestroika that he was finally able fulfil his dream.

Over the past few years, the last survivors from the town of Kamin have made contact with its present-day authorities. One of them, an Israeli by the name of Avraham Bieber, even organized an expedition to the town. In August of last year, a group of 14 people – most of whom were survivors from Kamin, journeyed there to search for the remains of their families. To their surprise, the town residents, who were mostly Ukrainian, had set up a nice welcome. Samuel Aba Kluman met some of his old comrades from the partisans.

The Elder Located the Grave

The goal of 68-year-old Klurman, however, was to reach Dovzhyk. No one seemed to know about the village, which had once been a mere 5 kilometers away from Kamin-Kashyrskyi. He questioned some of the town's oldest residents, and they informed him that Dovzhyk had been wiped off the face of the Earth. His extensive searching led him to two elderly women, one of whom used to work as a housemaid in the affluent Klurman family household. The woman was assisted by another elder, who confirmed that the Russians had indeed eradicated Dovzhyk. The 80-year-old agreed to help locate the place and led Klurman to where the house of Ivan had formerly stood. He said he well remembered that a family of seven had been murdered on that very spot. They located the grave with the help of the principal of a local school, a music teacher who lived nearby. He was a German-born former partisan who Aba Klurman had known from the war; upon digging up the grave, they discovered 7 skulls, of three adults and four children.

The adult skulls are thought to be those of the father David, the mother Menucha, and the maternal aunt Freidel, while the child ones are believed to be those of Klurman's 10-year-old sister Masha, his 7-year-old brother Yehoshua (Joshua), his four-year-old brother Tzvi, and Freidel's 8-year-old son Moshe. They were also identified by the set of gold teeth in the mouth of Menucha. Additionally, the pole Aba Klurman had planted in the ground was found close to the grave.

Transferred in a LOT Airplane to Lod Airport

The remains of the deceased, as well as shreds of clothing, were then placed in a crate and transferred in the mass grave of Kamin-Kashyrskyi victims. From that moment on, Klurman worked to bring them for reburial in Israel.

Last week, he finally fulfilled his dream: Klurman, his wife Sisel, and Kamin survivor Avraham Bieber traveled to Volyn Oblast together with Yeshayahu Kariv, an expert in the identification and transference of bodies. Kariv was asked to once again examine the claims regarding the identity of the skulls. Upon verifying their ages, the caskets were transported in a special truck up to the Russia-Poland border, under the escort of the mayor of Kamin.

At the annual memorial service for the Klurman-Dreitzen family, 1992.
Aba Klurman says Kaddish. At his side are his wife Sisel, Masha and Yehezkel.

The Klurman-Dreitzen family tombstone in the Qiryat Shaool cemetery in
Tel-Aviv.

28 I Get Closure

On my first trip to Kamin-Kashyrskyi, I tried to locate my goya, Anastasiya Gotsyk. My cousin Aba Klurman recalled it being called Karasin. I recalled it being called Karpilovka. After endless arguing, it turned out we were both right. The house was located on the borderline between the two villages. During the war, each of us had reached it from a different direction, and therefore thought of as being located in the village from which we came.

Aba remembered the way to the village, and thus we went back there. The house no longer stood there, but fortunately, as soon as we mentioned the names of Anastasiya Gotsyk and her son Pavluk, the locals knew who we were talking about. They told us that she had been murdered at the end of the war and that her son had passed away. They also said, however, that her daughter Vaska still lived in the village, and directed us to her house. To our disappointment, she had just traveled to the big city, and we were not able to meet her.

A heavy feeling filled my heart at the thought that my goya, who did so well by me, may have been murdered because someone discovered that she had harbored me. She may have paid with her life for the kindness she showed me.

These feelings would not leave my mind, and in August of 1993 I once again made the trip to Kamin-Kashyrskyi with Aba Klurman, his wife Sisel, and Avraham Bieber. This time I was joined by my daughter Limor and her husband Ron. It was very important to me to locate Anastasiya Gotsyk's daughter and find out what happened.

Aba, who couldn't join us that morning, drew Avraham Bieber a map showing how to reach the house. And so, I once again found myself knocking on the same house door. Vaska came out of the house and recognized me instantly! It was clear by the look in her eyes that she had absolutely no doubt about who I was. We hugged with all our might, flooded with tears.

Meeting her was intensely emotional and painful for me. The excitement engulfed us both. She turned to my daughter Limor and uttered, "Mashinka, Mashinka." She wasn't the first person to point out the strong resemblance between me and my daughter.

"Do you remember what was the first thing you requested of my mother, that night when she took you in?" she asked, and then continued: "Just make the itching go away."

She described how Anastasiya cut off my braids and told me she had kept them safe from harm up until the end of the war. She thought maybe someone from my family would one day show up looking for me, and she'd be able to give them my braids to remember me by. She didn't think I would survive after I left her home.

Surrounded by my daughter and her husband, sharing a hug with Vaska in her small home which bore a striking resemblance to the house in which her mother harbored me 51 years prior, with a lump in my throat and a flood of old memories coming back, I asked her to tell me what happened to her mother.

My good goya was murdered right before the end of the war by Ukrainian militia. They raided our village for food, as they had done countless times

The Ukrainian Insurgent Army – The UPA

The Ukrainian Insurgent Army (Ukrainian: Українська повстанська армія, УПА, Ukrayins'ka Povstans'ka Armiya, (UPA) were partisan units of the Nationalist Ukrainian Movement. They were known by many names, such as Banderists, Bulbovtsy, and more. They were founded by Ukrainian nationalists who felt they had been wronged by the Germans, who had broken their promise to let them establish an independent Ukrainian state on territories conquered from the Soviets. They murdered the Polish by the masses, burning down their villages and taking away their property. And of course, they also murdered any Jews they came across in the forest– however few of them still remained.

before, and shot her. Just because. No one ever knew she had rescued me, except for her aunt and children. She kept the secret until the day she died!

The pain in my heart for the loss of this good soul, without whom I do not believe I would be alive today, was adulterated by the relief of knowing that she did not die because of me, and her death was not on my conscience.

My renewed contact with Vaska would not break. Over the years I have sent her medicine, basic goods and money, in the hopes of repaying her, even by a little, for the months of grace and the great humanity her mother showed me when she harbored me during the four months of winter 1942-1943, by which she saved my life.

Throughout the years I always wished to grant Anastasiya Gotsyk the honorific of "Righteous Among the Nations[18]." I felt that her actions during those dark times, the way she opened her door and her heart to me while risking herself and her children to save me, made her worthy of the title.

As early as when the State of Israel was still in its infancy, I contacted the Yad Vashem institution, gave my testimony, and requested to initiate the process of granting her the honorific. I think I recall being told that a testimony from another person was required in order to verify my story. Throughout the years I made several more attempts, but to no avail.

The renewed relationship of steady correspondence I had established with Vaska in August of 1993 also extended to her daughter Nestia, a physician residing in Kiev. Since the collapse of the USSR, maintaining contact with her had become easier than with Karpilovka, which even today is a 16-hour train ride away from Kiev.

---

[18] The title of "Righteous Among the Nations (Hebrew: חֲסִידֵי אֻמּוֹת הָעוֹלָם, ḥasidei aumot HaOlam, lit. "righteous (plural) of the world's nations")" is an honorific granted by the State of Israel to non-Jews who risked their lives during the Holocaust to altruistically save Jews from extermination by the Nazis and their associates.

At some point, I asked Nestia to interview her mother and ask her what she remembered from that winter when I was in their home. To my astonishment, I received a long, detailed letter. Vaska and I are the same age, and our memories of that time overlapped!

With her letter serving as a supporting testimony to my spoken account recorded years earlier in Yad Vashem, I once again approached the institution, and this time, after a process of translation and a series of questions, I was granted the long-awaited permission.

The reunion with Vaska, daughter of Anastasiya Gotsyk. Ukraine, 1993

Accepting the certificate at the Shalom Aleichem Museum. Kiev, 2010

תעודת כבוד
ПОЧЕТНАЯ ГРАМОТА

Сим утверждается, что на заседании комиссии по присвоению звания Праведника народов мира, созданной при национальном институте памяти катастрофы и героизма Яд-Вашем, от 31·X·2010 на основе представленных свидетельств решено удостоить

Анастасию Гоцик

которая в годы фашистской оккупации рисковала своей жизнью ради спасения преследуемых евреев, звания Праведницы мира и наградить медалью Праведника народов мира.

Её имя будет высечено на Стене почета в Аллее праведников Яд-Вашем.

Иерусалим, Израиль
8 · XII · 2010

АВНЕР ШАЛЕВ
בשם רשות הזכרון יד ושם
ОТ ИМЕНИ ИНСТИТУТА ЯД ВА-ШЕМ

ЯКОВ ТЮРКЕЛЬ
בשם ועדה לציון חסידי אומות העולם
ОТ КОМИССИИ ПО ПРИСВОЕНИЮ ЗВАНИЯ ПРАВЕДНИК НАРОДОВ МИРА

In December of 2010, the Yad Vashem Institution finally recognized Anastasiya Gotsyk as a Righteous Among the Nations; her name will be forever inscribed on the Wall of Honor in the Garden of the Righteous Among the Nations in Holon.

On June 1, 2011 – 69 years after she risked her life to save my own, she was granted the honorific of Righteous Among the Nations in an emotional ceremony. Her entire extended family, my daughter Limor, and myself all had the honor of witnessing her daughter Vaska accept the certificate on her behalf, in the presence of representatives from Yad Vashem, Israel, Ukraine, and every religion in the country.

Several other certificates and honorifics were also granted in that ceremony, but I felt Vaska and I garnered the most attention because of the fact we were both standing there, bonded by fate through her mother's kind and compassionate heart.

For two days we stayed in Kiev under the hospitality of Nestia, and I dedicated every single minute of our stay to conversing with Vaska, who had come all the way from the village of Karpilovka, to glean every shred of our shared memory from that time long ago, trying in my heart and mind to reconcile the girl from I was back then with the woman I am today. These events exist only in the memories of the two of us, after all.

My daughter Limor once asked me where do I get the strength to return time and again to the soil of Poland, which has done so much to cast me out of its grounds. I tried to explain to her that though the trips cause me emotional turmoil and difficulty, they also give me strength and a sense of renewal.

73 years have passed, and after everything I had gone through, after everything I had been put through, I am here, alive! I return to my country of birth from the country where I truly belong, from my home, where I have a supportive partnership with my spouse and a loving family, to tell my story for the whole world to hear!

And it is precisely because it is happening here, on the soil of Poland, that it is so meaningful to me.

It is this feeling, this sense of strength, that I try to convey whenever I tell my story, whether it be in my lectures to various audiences every year on the Holocaust Remembrance Day (such as high school students, soldiers and the police), or in other ways, such as my participation in the March of the Living, my meetings with the Navy as part of a joint project of the IDF, the Amcha[19] organization and Ba'Alil Ltd, my involvement in creating a stage production based around my testimony, and an infinite number of other ventures.

Words cannot describe how proud I felt on the Holocaust Remembrance Day of April of 2016, when I was invited to the Knesset, the Israeli house of parliament, to light a candle as part of the annual memorial ceremony, with my two soldier grandchildren standing by my side on stage, and my entire family in the audience.

I lived.

I fulfilled Father's last wish.

---

[19] Amcha is an Israeli nonprofit-organization dedicated to supporting Holocaust survivors.

Yehezkel, My Husband and Partner

ראשון למרץ 1955

מאשה אהובה,

אהובתי היקרה, הפכתיני למנומר ועלי לצאת כאשר
צורארון חולצתי מורם אל על, או אולי ואכריזה
ואציג את מפעלך לראווה, את אשר אצרת בעדי מעשות
לך האזת ועשית לי. אולם אהבכתיך גם על כך.
ידעתי את אשר הציג סימן ליד. כזה כשפתי חמד,
אולם אין כשלך.

מתוך תקווה כי הכל שלום וכי ירד גשם בשדות אולם לא
יגרום לבוץ רב אשר יקשה עליך את דרכך אלי אני
האוהבך והעומד להתראות עמך בעוד יומיים מצפה כי
הופיעי גם באם יבוא המבול.

חיוך, קריצה, מבט מודי, חיוך מהלב ונשיקה.

רכושך
באהבה.

Yehezkel always looked out for me. When we married, I remember I said to myself… From this moment on, there is someone who will love me and take care of me... I knew he could see deep into my soul, that he understood how much I needed him. Yehezkel, my dear husband, the perfect gentleman, whose generosity knew no bounds. Always in a suit and tie, always well-groomed, always presentable.

Our life together was wonderful. My trust in him was absolute. I relinquished myself to him like I never did with anyone else. At his side I felt secure and safe. I felt at home.

As soon as we married, he began carving his professional way forward. In the beginning, he worked with his father in their family-owned glass workshop, while at the same time studying as well as working other jobs, in the evenings and even during the weekends. He stuck to his goal: to achieve financial independence and buy a house so he could give us a good life.

For a while he worked at Mekorot, Israel's national water company, and had a vehicle available to him as part of the job. Work had begun on setting up Israel's national water carrier at the time, and we took little Yaron on a trip to see the pipes being laid down in Ramot Menashe.

Work had just been completed on the Ramot Menashe tunnel, and the three of us, a young couple and a little baby, had a blissful time travelling along the green hills and taking in the enchanting smells of blossom. It is an image embedded deep in my memory and I will never forget that day.

I always knew that Yehezkel didn't just love me immensely, but also thought highly of me and valued my opinion. Above all, I knew he was proud of me, and liked to show and express this pride whenever he could. He enjoyed listening to others praise me and speak highly of me, and I felt that he even cared for me in a sort of fatherly way.

Any time he was invited to attend an event of any kind, he would always have me come along, no exception. His colleagues at the Technion Institute of technology knew that "if my wife isn't coming, neither am I" – and it wasn't rare for me to attend events with him where I was the only guest who wasn't part of the staff.

I was proud of him, too. His striving for excellence, the high level of responsibility with which he approached any endeavor, the way he climbed through the ranks at his workplace, the high-ranking positions he held and the success he had in every role he performed, his loyalty and dedication to his work, his professional ethics, and above all, the person he was: always listening, always generous and caring, never exhibiting an inkling of malice towards anyone. I have no doubt and would be willing to swear that never in his life did he hurt another human being.

I would observe him being such a great father to Yaron and Limor, how he valued every single detail, how he would half-jokingly say to them, "I don't care what grade you get in school, so long as it's an A+..." And they never let him down, always knowing that he was there for them to lean on as a firm beacon of support and security – a loving, caring father.

And what a wonderful Grandpa he was to our six grandchildren. Just as he took pride in the report cards of his own children, so too was he pride in those of his grandchildren. He would give them presents on his own birthday every year. Nothing made him happier than the act of giving.

He loved the country, he loved the army with its uniform and the prolonged periods of reserve duty and saw himself as a member of the founding generation, one who had fought without compromise for the independence of his home. He supported me completely when I decided to start volunteering in The Ghetto Fighters' House, when I stuck to my principles and refused to accept reparations from Germany[20], and when I started to tell the story of my days in the Holocaust. Just as he had pushed me to study and grow in our younger years, so too did he encourage me to participate in projects centered around the Holocaust, such as when I joined the March for the Living, and in all my other activity around the subject. "You need to continue", he would say to me encouragingly in times when I struggled with doubt and exhaustion, because he knew it was good for me and gave me an opportunity to tell my story and, through it, immortalize my beloved family.

After I retired, I became responsible for most household duties, while Yehezkel continued to work full-time at the Technion. Productivity was the most important thing in his eyes. He had little appreciation for those who did not work hard to achieve their goals. In fact, in all his years of working so diligently, he hardly ever got sick, and when he did, he never let it hinder his productivity.

Acts of injustice and corruption angered him greatly. As someone who grew up in the Irgun and fought hard to drive the British out of the Holy Land, he would sometimes sarcastically remark, "What a mistake… How could I drive them out… If only the British ruled here now, things would surely be different in this country of ours."

---

[20] As part of a treaty signed in the Postdam Conference after World War II, Germany agreed to pay reparations both to the State of Israel and the individual victims of the Holocaust living therein.

30 *Towards the End*

When he got sick in the summer of 2014, it didn't even register with me. We were so close and loved each other so much, we were virtually one being, and yet I never imagined those days would be our last. I was so used to the sense of wholesomeness we had in our shared life, to the security I felt whenever I was around him, that I just didn't see what was happening. He was more than my other half. He was everything.

I remember how after he was admitted to Carmel Hospital, we still talked about our plans, about traveling abroad, visiting museums and sightseeing, and what we'd do and how we'd do it… Having those casual, pleasant conversations seemed completely normal and made perfect sense to me.

And then he passed. It happened near the end of the holiday of Sukkot, on the 9th of October 2014.

And suddenly I discovered the vast, terrible void of being without him. The void which only keeps getting bigger and bigger as time goes on.

There isn't a morning when I don't find myself dreaming about our "us", our togetherness, about him doing the impossible and coming back home to the life we had. Dreaming that we go back to celebrating holidays together, to traveling and laughing and looking out for each other. Dreaming that he once again wears in his suit and we take the car to visit our grandchildren. Dreaming that we can go back to the pleasure of attending stage plays and concerts together, and continue to nurture the strong and wonderful relationship we have built together over more than sixty years.

I can hear him say to me… You'll manage, you know how to manage… And these warm words of affirmation lead me down the memory lane to my father, who also confidently told me that he had faith in me, that I'm strong and know how to manage… And just as I cried then, shaken and stricken with awe, so too do I cry now, struggling to accept – refusing to believe – that it's possible to be so alone.

In the days leading up to Yehezkel's death, I frequently prayed to my beloved grandmother, whom I've always believed to be listening to me and watching over me wherever I go, and whom I believe is still here today, despite the passage of time, to watch over me forever. I asked that she watch over him for me; I asked but couldn't change his fate.

The worst and most tormenting pain of all is knowing I was not there with him at midnight when it was all over. No one in the hospital had told me those were his final hours. I went home at around eight thirty in the evening and planned to return first thing in the morning. I even stayed up late, unaware of what was happening. I didn't begin to imagine what was to come, not saying a proper goodbye to him as I would have wished, not hugging him and telling him how painful his absence would be from now on.

Thankfully, he still fills the house with his presence, and his spirit is still very much with me. I go through drawers, examine documents and papers, read letters and notes, and see our shared life scattered around the house. To find comfort, to take a break from the pain and smile, I go back to reading the love letters he used to write to me in the first years of our marriage, or the fax messages and emails he sent me while I was staying in a hotel in Warsaw when I joined my grandson Yoad on the previously mentioned March of the Living in 2006.

"I missed you last night," he writes. "It is as though this is your first time being away. I am hopeful that you had a smooth landing and that none of you were caught in the pouring rain and left to wallow in the mud. Wear your volunteering proudly on your sleeve. I miss you greatly and announce as much to anyone who asks." And the date… February 28, 2006.

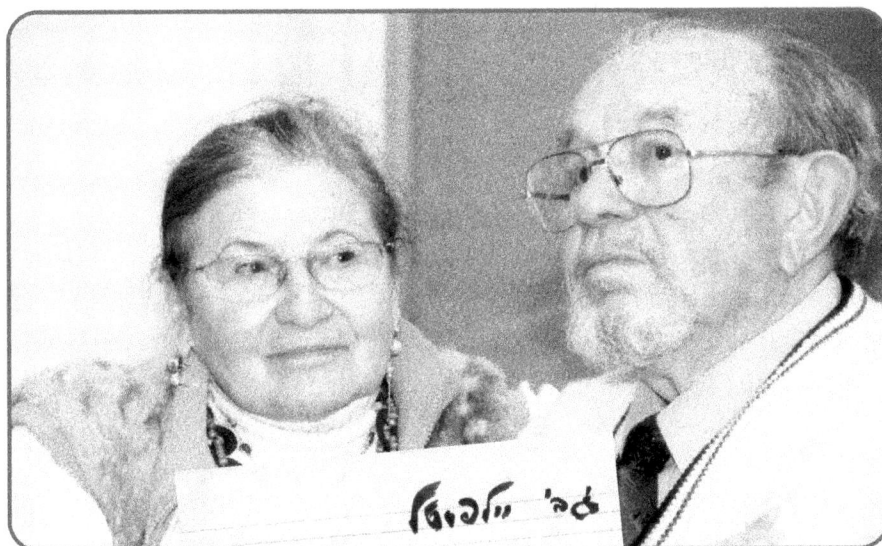

Letter reads:

MRS. WOLFSTHAL
I LOVE YOU

I was at home to pick up the computer.
I'm staying at work until late
(meeting with the president)
I had a sandwich.
Love
Y.

---

¹⁹ In reference to the president of the Technion Institute.

31 *The Family is My Life*

And now, I am learning to live in this new chapter of my life. I ask myself to muster up the strength to go back to my daily life, and once again find enjoyment in the good moments therein, such as the lectures I used to listen to at the Seniors' club, the physical exercises I used to do every Sunday, the English lessons I never missed, the testimonies I regularly gave about my experiences in the Holocaust – which I use as a way to heal from the wounds of the past – and above all: my family, which is the most precious thing to me in the entire world. To experience more and more of it, to relish as much as possible in the love and warmth it grants me.

There are many questions I still have to face… Should I leave my home, filled with so many fond memories, and move away from Haifa and closer to my daughter Limor? Do I choose to move into an assisted living home, in a new environment and a new way of life? How do I find the strength deep within to overcome the hardships and deal with the future to come?

Amidst my unrelenting sorrow which never lets up, and despite the tears still rolling down my cheeks, I think to myself that yes… I will soon be ready for the next stage.

My initial goal in writing this book was to tell my story, to put it to paper so that it can be eternally preserved in written form. The story of how I arrived here as a child without roots, and how I struck new roots and planted them firmly in the ground. It is here that I have gone through all stages of life. It is here that I have experienced love and parenthood, it is here that I have grown, built myself up, and have become the person who I am today – I am unequivocally and indisputably Israeli, and I belong in this land!

But now I feel like I'm writing it for Yehezkel. In his memory. To let the world know how much I loved him, how laudable and worthy our life together was, and how grand a miracle it was for me that fate had brought us together. What a shame that you didn't get to live to see this day.

This book is also my statement about my dear, wonderful family. A written testimony of my immense love for Yaron and Limor, my two fine, gifted, successful children whose mere existence has always been a remedy to my wounds, giving me copious amounts of joy and happiness, amplified even further by their relationships with their spouses Karin and Ron, and the lovely families they have built with them.

And this book is an opportunity to proudly call out the names of my perfect grandchildren: Yoad, Lior, Yotam, Yarden, Shay, and Nimrod, and tell them that on the day they were born, the world became full of wonderful reasons to get up every morning and witness its mesmerizing beauty. Each one of you is remarkably handsome, loved to no end, smart and intelligent, multi-talented, a true source of my joie de vivre, for many wonderful moments of excitement, laughter, magic, and a love for this land.

Thank you for being here with me. You are all a continuous source of pride for me. I am overjoyed to watch you grow and evolve, acquiring education, always learning, always active and always loved. May you succeed in everything you do, be happy and content, fulfill all your dreams and always keep your love for each other and the beautiful share.

Memory and love – that's what it's all about. I love you, I love this land, and pray that we may continue to strike deep roots into its soil.

From right to left: standing – Limor, Yoad, Yaron, Shay, Lior, Karin, Rachel, Yarden, Pazit.
Seated – Yehezkel, Nimrod, Masha, Yotam.

My 80th Birthday

Limor and I wanted to say a few words to our mother –

the grandmother of our children and the close friend of everyone here.

Mom – there are two traits, two central themes, two words that could describe you:

Strength and love.

They are tightly twined together within you, and anyone who knows you knows them well.

The first time the world saw your strength was when you were still just a child. Against all odds, in the face of all the horrors of World War II and the Nazi machine of destruction, you made your resolve to live. It is a story well-known to everyone sitting here.

And anyone who knows you is also familiar with the other side that completes the first – that is, your ability to recover, build yourself up and build up your family, strengthening us all with pure love. That's how it's always been – you have always looked ahead. Your love was what gave us the strength to be where we are today. Limor and I hope that we've learned those things from you – to find those qualities within ourselves and give our families the love which you have given us... And if that is the one thing we have managed to learn from you – why, that is more than enough.

There are countless examples, stories and anecdotes that could be pointed to for proof of the strength and love you have in your heart, which you have shared with all of us. If I had to pick one example, it would have to be the way you have become a paragon of virtue to the younger generation as well – from school-aged youth to the soldiers in the IDF which you continue to work with to this day.

In conclusion, may you continue to grant us, Grandpa, and all members of the extended family and the entire State of Israel with strength and love, for many, many years to come...

From your loving family,
4.29.2011

The family's greeting to Masha on her 80th anniversary

April 29, 2011

Dear family members,

First, I must say that the idea to gather here today to celebrate my birthday was Limor and Ron's, bless their hearts. Happy birthday greetings are in order for Limor as well, who is also celebrating hers today.

Tonight is a very special and momentous night for me, and happy too; it's not every day that one celebrates eighty years of life.

And I shall start from the end.

Two days ago, Grandpa and I were present for our beautiful granddaughter Lior's Officers Course graduation ceremony, where she received her officer's pin, cementing her new rank within the IDF. This event made me proud, happy, and joyous beyond words, and for that she has my gratitude and my respect.

And now, a tiny bit of reminiscence, even if everyone here is familiar with most of the story.

A couple of days ago, my grandson Yotam asked me: "Savta, how was your assimilation into Israel?"

The truth is it's a tough question to answer. I think my reply to Yotam was that my happiest moments from that time were my wedding to Grandpa and the births of my children.

In his sensitivity, Yotam noted that I always see the glass half-full, and I think that is indeed correct.

I have been reminiscing about my childhood lately – about Mother, and Father, and my home; on one hand there are the good memories, and on the other, the ones from the war. One particularly strong memory is our liberation at the end of the war. Everyone is celebrating – hugging, kissing and cheering – but I find it difficult to celebrate.

During the war we had awaited victory, and when it finally came, our happiness was not without sadness. I was a child all alone, grown up prematurely, with no home, no family, and no one to share the victory with. I had nothing. Nothing but Father's will: "You need to live, and you will live." And so, I tried with all my might to cling to life, to heed Father's command, which stays with me to this day.

The road I had been walking had not been a bed of roses, but I had a goal: to carry on and reach the destination of the Land of Israel.

Masha's speech on her 80th anniversary

I believed we would be greeted with a red carpet as soon as we disembarked from the ship. So came my first disappointment – there was no red carpet. There was, however, Kibbutz Dafna, which had prepared a warm and gracious welcome for the children who had come from the inferno. It was in the days prior to the War of Independence, when the Hagana, Palmach and Irgun were still fighting to establish an independent Jewish state in The Land of Israel.

There was a Palmach base in Kibbutz Dafna, and watching its members in their training, we desperately wanted to be like them: to fight for the liberation of the Land, to belong in the Land and contribute to the efforts of establishing the new country. We had considerable success in that regard and were proud to be among its founding members. We built a new kibbutz bordering with Syria on the north, known today as Kibbutz Gadot. Life wasn't easy, but it brought with it much pride. We lived in the present. We had a future.

My aspirations, however, were different: to leave the kibbutz, to study, to serve in the army, to start a family. And I followed those aspirations through, leaving the kibbutz to study in Giv'at HaShlosha college and becoming a certified kindergarten teacher. After I graduated, I joined the IDF and served a full two years of mandatory service – but still, I did not have a family of my own.

And then, one night, he showed. Not a knight in shining armor, but a man with a loving heart nonetheless. We click. We love each other. We have plans for the future, then a family, a continuation of the generational chain. We share many joys together, big and small alike. My son Yaron is born – what bliss! And then my daughter Limor – and our bliss is doubly great! Our family progresses one step at a time, and the children are growing up. They study diligently at school, always bringing home excellent report cards. They graduate and join the army, both achieving the rank of Officer. Our pride is immense. And I'd be remiss not to mention the participation of Yehezkel and the children in many of the wars throughout the history of our country, and how concerned I was for their safety whenever they were drafted.

The years go by, and both children graduate from the Technion and leave the nest. The generational chain continues, however, as they marry and start wonderful families. And as the family tree grows greater and greater, so does our joy.

Our beautiful grandchildren come along, bringing us just as much pride as they grow older and older – and only we remain young, at heart and in spirit.

Yoad has recently been discharged from the army after a full three years of service and is now looking to the future ahead. Lior has just graduated the Navy's Officers' Course, and her way is paved for a great future as well. And we – Grandpa and I – are there for every step of the way, sharing in the joys for their accomplishments. Every time we get a phone call from any of our grandchildren, we are filled with pride: we are remembered.

I am sitting here tonight, surrounded by the family I have built with your father and grandfather Yehezkel, and I love what I see. I am grateful for all the blessings I have been bestowed, for having reached this moment, and for all that I've got: wonderful children with wonderful spouses, I and six beautiful grandchildren, to continue the chain for generations to come.

Amidst this great joy, however, there is a corner in my heart for my hometown, and for those who were not as fortunate as I. I have fulfilled my father's will – Father, I am alive!

With a prayer in my heart: "Dear Lord, please let our sons, and the sons of our sons, and the generations to follow, leave in peace in this land."

A big thanks to my husband, who is with me through the good and the not-so-good, always supporting me to this day.

And a big thanks and a happy birthday to my beautiful daughter Limor, her husband Ron and to everyone who came here to share in our joy.

33 *Appendices*

1. Cenotaph in Memory of the Jewish Community of Kamin-Kashirsky and the Vicinity at the Holon Cemetery

2. A Grave Monument in Memory of the Kamin-Kashyrskyi Ghetto

3. Gravestone Erection Ceremony in Commemoration of the Burial Site of the Jews of Kamin-Kashyrskyi

4. Masha's Speech at the Annual Klurman-Dreitzen Memorial Service, Tel-Aviv, October 1994

5. The March of the Living in Poland with my Grandson Yoad and his Grade in Winter 2007

6. The March of the Living – Letter from a Group of School Students

7. Navy Project – December 2010

8. Letter from School Teacher Yuval Kahn

9. Masha's Speech at the "Righteous Among the Nations" Award Ceremony, Kiev, Ukraine - June 2011

10. VeHee SheAmda: on Three Women who Prevailed

11. Letter of Appreciation from Israeli Police Division 534

12. Certificate of Merit from the State of Israel

13. Letter of Appreciation from Head of the Research Division – IDF Intelligence Corps

14. Letter of Appreciation from Unit 8200

15. Letter of Gratitude from Ghetto Fighters' House

16. Invitation to Light a Memorial Candle at the Knesset

17. Forest of the Martyrs

Cenotaph in Memory of the Jewish Community of Kamin-Kashirsky and the Vicinity at the Holon Cemetery

A Grave Monument in Memory of the Kamin-Kashyrski Ghetto

1942 ✡ **1992**

Here stood the ghetto of
Kamin-Kashyrskyi
and the vicinity,
inhabited by around
3000 Jews who were sent
to their deaths on the
following dates:

א' ר"ח אלול תש"א - 8.23.1941
כ"ז מנ' אב תש"ג - 8.10.1942
כ"ב מר חשוון תש"ג - 11.2.1942

Others escaped into the forests
to fight in the ranks of the
partisans.

Honored be their memory!

Gravestone erection ceremony at the burial site of around 100 of Kamin-Kashyrskyi's Jews murdered before the termination of the ghetto – Kamin-Kashyrskyi, August 1993

Masha's Speech at the Annual Klurman-Drajcen Memorial Service, Tel Aviv, October 3 , 1994

My family, dear friends, and honorable guests,

We gather here today to remember and remind.

Despite the passage of time, we do not forget our loved ones who are not with us anymore.

Even if our daily lives demand our fullest attention and dedication to present day affairs, when the Day of Remembrance draws near, it is as though the present temporarily fades away and the past returns full force.

A whole host of strong and faded emotions held within us all these years comes out bursting all at once, and it is as if the pain and longing for our loved ones suddenly becomes more intense, and their loss is felt strongly in every joy and every sorrow.

But they are always deep within our hearts. And as the past moves farther and farther away, the memories of them only become clearer and more vivid; and while time may dull the pain, it is never forgotten. Indeed, we must not forget! All those who survived have a duty to remember and remind!

We stand here today at this cemetery, so few of us, only a minute number of survivors from large, glorious, expansive families. We are the survivors of the inferno. Standing by our side are the families we ourselves have built – our children and grandchildren – and together we honor the memory of those who did not survive, who did not have the fortune to grow up and taste the taste of life, even though so much of it was still ahead of them. Their lives were cut short by an evil, malevolent hand; some of them were mere infants, while others were full-grown adults and even elderly. They were our children, our parents, our grandfathers and our grandmothers.

On this day of commemoration, more than half a century has gone by. Precisely 52 years ago today, November 2nd, 1942, was the last day of the Kamin-Kashyrskyi ghetto. That was the day the Nazis declared death on the last of the Jews therein.

But we, a minute few, were blessed with the opportunity to raise families, to build new homes and be among the founders of a new country in a new land, feeling new lives starting within us. God only knows the whos and whats of why we were the ones bestowed with this blessing. Perhaps it was thanks to the sacrifices of those that were not.

But there will always be a gut-wrenching feeling in our hearts, wondering "what if they were also..."

Today we stand here without words, each of us absorbed in their own memories, as images appear and promptly disappear. Some pleasant, some of abrupt endings.

But despite it all, we are here today with our families and with our children and grandchildren. We who did not have the fortune of knowing grandpa and grandma, who grew up without uncles, aunts and cousins, gave birth to children who grew up in a different reality. In the shadow of a dark era which we tried so hard to keep away and hide from them, they are now the ones who support us, who want to know, who do not disconnect themselves from the past. They are our pride and joy, the continuation of the chain, they are the generations to succeed our own! They are the continuation that our parents prayed for as they went to their deaths.

Let us not forget those who were not brought to a proper burial in the Land of Israel, whose remains are still scattered in unknown places, and let us carry a silent prayer in our hearts that someday they will be located and given a proper burial in Israel.

Every year since this grave monument was erected, I have come here and stood in awe as the image of the Dovzhyk forest appeared before me, connecting everything back to that time, to those days so distant, yet so vivid – the small dirt mound, the smells, the sounds, and the electrifying tension in the air. Aba, Sisel, Archik, his late wife and myself have located the remains of our relatives with the help of a gentile man who said he would show us the way. He walks about confidently, and we are left dumbstruck at his words. A difficult experience leaves us all aghast.

Another experience of mine: It's the last day in the ghetto, an autumn morning in a pleasantly breezy November, my father walks briskly under the bright, blue sky, and with my small hand in his, I do my best to keep up. I look around, breathing in the fresh air, blinded by the light of day; like all the children who were still alive in the ghetto at that point – however few there still were – I had been staying in the basement for months. My father and I arrive at the gate of the ghetto and walk through. This was my first and last time walking through the gate. Left behind in the ghetto were my mother and little brother Moisha'le, as well as the few relatives of Aba Klurman and myself who were still alive.

Today we have the fortune of seeing their remains reburied here.

For the fourth year in a row, we gather at this monument on the Kamin-Kashyrskyi Memorial and Mourning Day, and we do not forget how blessed we are for having borne witness to the day when remains of our loved ones are brought to proper burial in Israel. And for that we have to thank Aba, Sisel and Avraham Bieber, who committed themselves to this goal with great dedication and resolve, taking considerable risks to achieve it.

On this day, we commemorate the memory of all the Jews of Kamin-Kashyrskyi and the entire Volyn Oblast who were not blessed to be brought to proper burial in Israel.

Thank you all for coming today and honoring us and with your presence, and a thank you to the people whose hard work and unwavering devotion allowed us to see this day.

The March of the Living in Poland
with My Grandson Yoad and his Grade in Winter 2006

The extent of the evils and atrocities committed here, on the soil of Poland, would be difficult to put into words.

Poland, my country of birth, where 3.5 million Jews lived before the war, is not a country to return to in joy. It is not a homeland, not a home.

It is a country filled with memorials and crematoriums.

And in these times, when there are those who would deny that the Holocaust ever happened, we who remain, who were there, must pass on to you, our children and grandchildren, the knowledge of what happened, of what we saw with our own two eyes, and what we felt and as we did.

even if the mind refuses to comprehend – there indeed was a Holocaust.

The black stones here tell the story, and the gas chambers cry out: "Do Not Forget Us!"

Let us remember the one million children. They all had hopes and dreams just like all of you, but they did not get to fulfil those dreams.

All of us – you and your parents, who were born into an independent country, as well as I – are fortunate to have been blessed to have a land, a state and a flag to call our own. I pray along with you that we shall always protect it, uphold it, and know that we have no other homeland.

You are our future, and I am proud to be here among you. I believe most of you will spread your wings and reach the stars. And somewhere in your heart, you will always remember you were here and saw with your own eyes what happened before we had our own homeland.

Speech given by Masha during the trip to Poland, March 2006

The March of the Living 2007
Letter from a Group of School Students

3.3.2007

First of all, many **Mazal Tov** wishes for your birthday.

This is not just any birthday, but the birthday of a truly remarkable woman.

We know you were probably planning to be in Israel on your birthday, celebrating with your children and grandchildren, but life has led you here, to tell us your story, and we feel blessed for having had the opportunity to go on this journey and hear it from you.

Masha,

While only 4 days have passed since the beginning of this journey, we feel you have managed to really reach our hearts and convey your feelings and emotions from the time of the war.

Though you are small, you are absolutely **larger than life!**

Through your story we got to know the beauty of your character: You are a fighter, you are strong, you are determined – in short, you are a hero!!!

We wish you all the best, a whole lot of bliss, good health and positive experiences galore.

Hope you will always be happy.

We really think this journey wouldn't be the same without you!

Happy Birthday!

Love always

The "grandkids"
Group 5 and the chaperons.

We have added a special gift
which represents you:
free and full of different colors
Hope you like it!

Navy Project   December 2010

In a 2010 initiative by the IDF's YALTAM unit Divers' Course command, a group of Divers' Course cadets met with ten Holocaust survivors for a series of weekly 90-minute sessions in which they listened to their stories about their experiences from the Holocaust. The project was coordinated by Sharon Wolf and directed by Tzvika Apple, who managed to bridge between the generations with sensitivity and humility. The soldiers listened, documented, and wrote down our stories.

As a token of appreciation for our participation in the project, we were all invited to the course graduation ceremony. Having proudly served in the Navy myself, I was deeply moved by the impressive ceremony, as the sight of the submarine docking at the port and the white-uniform soldiers brought my memories from my own time in the IDF back to the surface.

בבקרים הם השיטו צוללות, בערבים הם אספו עדויות מניצולי שואה

צללו לזיכרונות

חניכי קורס הצוללנים של חיל הים החליטו להקדיש את השעות המעטות הפנויות שעמדו לרשותם כדי להיפגש עם ניצולי שואה ולתעד את סיפוריהם ● "הקורס קשה, אבל כששמענו מה עבר עליהם – הכל התגמד"

דוד רגב | כתבנו לענייני רווחה

Yediot Aharonot, December 12, 2010

Diving into the Memories

IDF YATLAM[22] Divers' Course cadets dedicate what little free time they have from rigorous training to meet with Holocaust survivors and document their stories. 'The course has been tough, but having listened to what the survivors went through, we realize our struggles dwarf in comparison'.

David Regev | Published in Israeli daily newspaper Yediot Aharono

Between the grueling physical exercises and complex qualification courses, a group of submariners devoted themselves to documenting the stories of 10 Holocaust survivors.

Hundreds of people filled the Haifa naval base on Sunday to watch the graduation ceremony of the prestigious IDF Submarine Divers' Course. Among the attendants were 10 proud and excited guests not related by blood to any of the new graduates.

Those were ten Holocaust survivors, all residing in Haifa, who had been an inseparable part of this year's course. Over the past three months, they spent long hours meeting with the cadets and sharing their experiences from the ghettos, concentration camps and death camps with them, while the soldiers put their accounts to paper, preserving them for posterity.

This unique initiative was conceived by the IDF Naval high command and supervised by the Divers' Course commander. The high command decided that in addition to the regular training Divers' Course cadets are required to go through each year, this year's young soldiers would also undertake a task of great value to society at large – the documentation of the experiences of Holocaust survivors.

"Throughout the project, ten cadets were paired with ten survivors in order to document their stories so that they could be passed down to future generations," said Sharon Wolf, Deputy Director of the Amcha organization Haifa branch, who served as coordinator of the project.

"Despite the great pressure they were under, the cadets' performance was exemplary."

Continued next page

---

[22] The YALTAM unit (Hebrew acronym for "יְחִידָה לְמָשִׁימוֹת תַּת-יְמִיּוֹת", lit. "Unit for Underwater Missions" is [according to English Wikipedia:] "a defensive divers unit tasked with mine countermeasures, explosive ordnance disposal and salvage and recovery." Referred to in English as "Unit for Underwater Fighting".

The special documentation process, which was completed just days ago, included written and visual material. The cadets also devoted what little free time they had during the course to producing a special booklet and computer disc with all the stories they had accumulated.

"They are our new grandchildren," described Sarah Meirovitz, 70, a Holocaust survivor from Romania as she excitedly talked about 'her diver'. "I am so proud to see him graduate the course. He was deeply moved by my story."

Cadet M, who documented Sarah's memories, wouldn't stop thanking her yesterday for coming to his graduation. "At first we were rather apprehensive about meeting the survivors. We didn't know how they'd react and weren't sure they would want to tell us what they had been through," he explained.

"But Sarah and her friends were very welcoming. We could see it was important to them to share their stories with us. It was really heartwarming." It was very important to M. to introduce Sarah to his family. "The course has been tough, but hearing what survivors went through, we realize our struggles dwarf in comparison'.

"I was 11 when we fled the Nazis in Hungary," said 77-year-old Haim Sorek, another survivor. "I told the diver I met everything I had experienced there. I am sure we will stay in touch in the future."

In light of the project's success, naval high command and the Amcha organization are planning to continue with the initiative in future courses.

The original article as appeared in the newspaper.
Originally written and translated by David Regev; translation edited by Yotam Wolfsthal

Letter from School Teacher Yuval Kahn

Dear Masha!

The reason I have not written to you earlier is that things have been slowly brewing up in my heart ever since the day I had the honor of meeting you in Ghetto Fighters' House. Since you were so open and up front with us, I'll allow myself to also write to you in an open and informal manner. I have been a teacher at the Hartman High School in Jerusalem for seven years now. During this time, I have gotten to hear the witness reports of many Holocaust survivors. Never before had I been able to so strongly identify with the person speaking in front of me, to feel so close to them. Your touching, intimate way of sharing your story creates a direct connection between you and your audience. The students I spoke with after the meeting felt the same way. We were all captivated by your personal charm and feel grateful for the chance of meeting you.

As a teacher and as a parent, it has been particularly fascinating to me to compare the impact your story had on me to its impact on our students. Our students were particularly enthralled by the viewpoint of you as a child and the difficult adventures you had to endure at such a young age. As for me, I was completely engrossed in the character of your father, which you have described in such a gentle yet rich manner. His character has led me to reflect on my own character, both as a son and as a father. I was particularly impressed by how much your father valued his children's education, and by how practical he was, as shown by the preparations he made before occupation, and by the way he fulfilled his role as the patriarch of the family during the time of the war.

What I found the most thought provoking was of course the way your father took care of you before the war began, as well as when it was already underway. The instructions he gave you, his faith in you, the sense of confidence he instilled in you. You managed to very clearly convey to us the conflict you felt, as a child and an adult, about his decision to leave you alone in the forest – a decision which put your life at great risk but was also the thing that ultimately saved it. The average person cannot begin to imagine how it feels to be in situations like this, which I hope no one ever has to experience; but you did, and not only that, but you also agreed to share with us what you went through.

In doing so, you have allowed us a glimpse into the depths of the human soul, into dark and terrible places, where fear and despair exist side by side with mighty powers of survival and a burning desire to live.

In your story, you left the conflict as it was, unresolved, so visceral, so impactful, so deep and so real, that it has stayed with me ever since, and I believe it will stay with me for years to come. I pray I will never have to face such a conflict, but I know those deep feelings are not just relevant to the most dramatic and extreme scenarios, but also to our simple, daily lives.

I wish to thank you from the bottom of my heart for everything mentioned above. I shamefully admit that until now I have never sat down to write a letter to a Holocaust survivor after listening to their testimony. Even this simple human duty is something I have learned from you, dear Masha.

I wish you and your family many years of health and strength, and I wish for myself and for my future students to have the honor of meeting you again.

On behalf of my students and myself,

best regards,

Yuval Kahn

Masha's Speech at the Righteous Among the Nations Award Ceremony, Kiev, Ukraine

Wednesday, June 1, 2011

Representatives of Yad VaShem, the Israeli delegation, distinguished Guests, family of the late Anastasiya Gotsyk and my daughter Limor.

I am deeply honored to be here today, in Kiev, the capital of Ukraine, for this heartfelt and unforgettable ceremony, in the Shalom Aleichem museum, named after the well-known Yiddish author born in this very city.

I am eternally grateful to the kind and wonderful family of the late Nastia, her daughter Vaska, her granddaughter Nestia and the members of their household.

I am overwhelmed by a flood of emotions as I remember this noble and generous woman, who knowingly risked her life and the life of her family to take me into her home in those dark, twisted times.

It was the end of December 1942 going into 1943. Winter had just about reached its peak. It hadn't started snowing yet, but it was very cold.

The war was in full swing, and the Germans were advancing into the heart of Russia. And there I was, a child about 10 or 11 years old, wandering the villages of the region all by myself. I was hungry, underdressed, riddled with lice, and desperate for just a bit of warmth.

And then, like a gift from The Heavens, one door opened to reveal a wonderful woman, who instead of pushing me away like everyone else, took me into her home, fed me, bathed me, cut my lice-riddled braids, and dressed me up in the clothes of Vaska, who is present here today, and with whom I have maintained close contact ever since I reunited with her several years ago.

I was very happy to be able to return to the village of Karpilovka several decades later, to finally thank the family who had saved me from the jaws of the freezing cold and the death lurking for me in every corner.

I was not free to walk around the house. I had to stay in the pantry to avoid being discovered by the neighbors or by the Poltavan teacher lodging with the family.

Every morning, dear Nastia would cover me with warm clothes to keep me from freezing and then quietly lead me into the pantry, imploring me to keep very silent, lest anyone heard a noise and realized there was someone hiding somewhere in the area. And every evening, she would take me back in to warm up on the hearth on which I slept.

Even when the Germans and their collaborators raided the village, she managed to outwit them, and in her great resourcefulness, keep me out of their hostile gaze.

In the beginning of spring 1943, completely by chance, my partisan cousin arrived at her home and found me there, upon which he had his comrade bring me to the woods. It was then that I was informed that my entire family had been murdered.

When the borders of the USSR were opened to Israeli travelers, I began my search for the family of Nastia. in 1991 finally reunited with Vaska in her hometown of Karpilovka, which was also when I met Nestia for the first time.

Vaska told me that after I had left their home, her mother cried over me since she didn't think I would survive. After all, the war was still in full swing in 1943. Aside from Vaska and her brother Pavluk, no one in the village or in the surrounding area knew I was harbored in their house. Their mother had strictly forbidden them from mentioning me to anyone.

I had been trying to locate them ever since the war ended but had had no success. Only on that day in 1991, five decades after her mother had harbored me in their home, we were finally able to meet again by the grace of God Almighty, both of us now grandmothers with families of our own

As joyful as the meeting was, however, It was also sad, as I learned that Mrs. Nastia had been murdered by the Nazis and Pavluk had died in the army. And today we meet again in this respectable, emotional and joyous event.

I am thankful to Yad Vashem for having found Miss Nastia Gotsyk worthy of being included in the pantheon of the Righteous Among the Nations. I am thankful for everyone who had a hand in this decision. I thank the Israeli Embassy for inviting me to this joyous event, and a great, sincere thank you to this magnificent family.

Masha Wolfsthal

VeHee SheAmda[23]
On Three Women Who Prevailed

Photos from a stage production by Beit Ivshitz in Haifa in which I was involved behind the scenes as a Holocaust survivor. Over the course of several months, I, along with two other survivors, met with a group of teenagers participating in the "No'ar Ne'eman LeZichron HaShoa" project (Hebrew: נוֹעַר נֶאֱמָן לְ זִיכְרוֹן הַ שׁוֹאָ ה lit. Youth Loyal to the Memory of the Holocaust") and told our story.

Our testimonies were later adapted into a stage show which we had an active role in developing together with the students.

The show was presented in Haifa on June 2, 2013.

Written by: Yael Englander
Directed by: Hagit Bar
Initiative and mentorship: Hava Alter

12. 11. 13   בס"ד

למאושה היקרה...

אנו מחלקת שח"מ **538.13** רוצים לספר אותך
בנסיעות שבו ואזו הנו בהזקבות סיפור חייך.
אין לנו דרך לתאר את תחושת ההזדבה שלנו
כלפייק. כולדה שמחת לבדק את קשייק במלחמה
הקשה מכל, מלחמה שקמה בהזקבות שלזות
חינך עם הבטון הטוכיבי כלפי הזוכרחיק
היהדים.

ביזיה שתוק מאסמבתתק כאר אינת וגורל של התחלק
השו אונו יצות,

אנו מאריביק אותק על הובון לפאמשיק לחיות אם ההשרותק
כולה הזצורות, אנו אוהים כק שהבקאסר מאצמנק
ושאימא אותנו הסיפורק הרוישי, אך הרבון
להתגבר על מכשולי הדרק כך הזיותק זה

וזו כק שמרות האומצות (שורת ואמנק
הירבותק לאמאק כק הזיזיה שבי יכול לצלות חייק?

התברת הנו את הכאוה הדרות חזק מבלמ
היהדי. והתור שורים לקן לשמור על האנינה
שלנו.

– כי אין לנו עולם אחרת –

באוהבה, הצרבה
והצריכ
בטוב
❤️ מא 538

November 12, 2013

Dear Masha...

We here at division 534 were all deeply touched by your life story and would like to tell you about some of the thoughts and feelings it has left in us.

We cannot begin to describe how much we admire you. As a mere child you were forced to stand on your own against adversity amidst the most terrible war of all time. A war which never would have broken out if it weren't for the Nazi regime's gratuitous hatred towards its Jewish citizens.

We marvel at your strong resolve to stay alive and keep on fighting, knowing that half of your family is gone and the fate of the other half is uncertain; at your ability to overcome any obstacle despite your young age. We also laud your choice to stay true to your Judaism and to your people despite all the hardships you had been through, even when you knew it could cost you your life.

You have made us proud to be a part of the Jewish people, keeping our country safe as officers of the law.

For we have no other country!

> With love,
> admiration,
> and much appreciation,
>
> **Division 534**

Certificate of Merit from the State of Israel

מדינת ישראל
משרד החינוך

תעודת הוקרה

מוענקת בכבוד רב

לאשת העדות

וולפסטל מאשה

על פעילותך ותרומתך הרבה
בהנחלת זיכרון השואה והגבורה
בקרב בני הנוער וחיילי צה"ל ומפקדיו

במעשיך אלו הבטחת
כי דור המחר לעולם
"יזכור ולא ישכח"

יישר כוח!

הרב
שי פירון
שר החינוך

רב – אלוף
בנימין (בני) גנץ
ראש המטה הכללי

חנוכה, תשע"ד, נובמבר 2013

This Certificate of Appreciation
Is Honorably Granted To

Mrs. Masha Wolfsthal

For your continuous activity and extensive
contribution to the cause of passing down the memory
of the Holocaust to Israel's youth, and the soldiers and
commanders of the Israel Defense Force.

Your efforts have guaranteed that our future
generation will "remember and never forget."

WELL DONE!

Lieutenant General
Benjamin (Benny) Ganz
Commander in Chief

Rabbi
Shai Piron
Minister of Education

Hanukkah, November 2013

Letter of Appreciation from Head of the Research Division
IDF Intelligence Corps

כ"ד ניסן תשע"ה
13 באפריל 2015

תעודת הוקרה

לגב' משה וולפסטל

על תרומתך לשימור זיכרון השואה והנחלתו לדורות הבאים, בכך ששיתפת את סיפורך האישי עם משרתי חטיבת המחקר.

בהוקרה והערכה,

אלי בן מאיר, תת אלוף
רח"ט המחקר

April 13, 2015

This Certificate of Appreciation

for

Mrs. Masha Wolfsthal

For your contribution to the preservation of the memory of the Holocaust by passing it down to future generations, by sharing your personal story with the soldiers and officers of the Research Division.

With Recognition and Appreciation,

Eli Ben-Meir, Brigadier General

Head of the Research Division

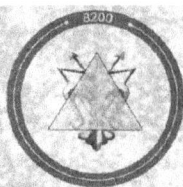

תעודת הוקרה

מוענקת בזאת ל:

מאשה וולפסטל

על תרומתך לשימור זיכרון השואה

והנחלתו לדורות הבאים

נועם שער, אל"מ

מפקד המרכז

Integration Center

This Certificate of Appreciation

is Hereby Granted to

Masha Wolfsthal

for your contribution

to the preservation

of the memory of the Holocaust

by passing it down

to future generations

Colonel Noam Shaar

Commander of Center

Letter of Gratitude from Ghetto Fighters' House

בית לוחמי הגטאות
ע"ש יצחק קצנלסון למורשת השואה והמרד

מאשה היקרה

הבעת תודה והערכה

בשם עובדי בית לוחמי הגטאות ברצוני להביע את תודתנו
והערכתנו על התנדבותך רבת השנים.

במשך שנים ובמסירות רבה פגשת קבוצות תלמידים ומבוגרים כדי
לספר להן על קורותייך וקורות משפחתך בתקופת השואה, כילדה
צעירה שנותרה בודדה בעולם. סיפרת להם על המפגש עם הרוע
האנושי אך גם עם אנשים טובים שהושיטו לך יד.

בחרת להדגיש אמירות ערכיות-הומניות אשר נגעו לשמירת ערך
האדם, ליכולת לשמור על צלם אנוש ולקבל את הזולת, האחר
והשונה.

המסר והקול הייחודי שלך נגעו בלבות המאזינים וסייעו להם לנסות
ולהבין ולו במעט את אשר חווית בתקופת השואה.
תרמת תרומה משמעותית לבית לוחמי הגטאות ולכל מבקר,
תלמיד או חייל שפגש אותך במהלך השנים.

אנו נפרדים ממך בהכרת תודה גדולה על פועלך ומאחלים לך
בריאות טובה, הנאה ונחת מהמשפחה

בברכה,
דורקה שטרנברג,
צוות ההדרכה
ועובדי המוזיאון בבית לוחמי הגטאות

במרכז הלימודי בבית לוחמי הגטאות עם חיילי גולני

The Ghetto Fighters' House
The Itzhak Katzenelson Holocaust
and Jewish Resistance Heritage Museum,
Documentation and Study Center

Expression of Gratitude and Appreciation

Dear Masha,

On behalf of the employees of the Ghetto Fighters' House, I would like to express my gratitude and appreciation for your many years of volunteering with us.

For many years, you have devoted yourself to meeting with groups of students and adults alike to share the story of yourself and your family in the Holocaust as a young child left alone in the world. You've told them about your encounters with the evil of man, but also with kind people who lent you a helping hand.

You have chosen to center your testimony around messages of the value of life, the acceptance of others regardless of race, nationality or beliefs, and not losing one's humanity in a world twisted by hate.

Your message and unique voice have touched the hearts of your audience, and helped your listeners get some form of understanding, however partial, of your experiences in the Holocaust.

You have contributed greatly to both The Ghetto Fighters House and to every visitor, student and soldier who have met you over the years.

We bid you farewell with deep gratitude for your endeavors and wish you the best of health, and much happiness with your family.

All the Best

Dorke (Dor) Sternberg
The Staff of Instructors
And all employees of the
Ghetto Fighters' House

Invitation to Light a Memorial Candle at the Knesset

בס"ד

יושב-ראש הכנסת
Speaker of the Knesset

ירושלים,יום שלישי, כ"ה ניסן, תשע"ה
14 אפריל 2015

לכבוד
הגב' מאשה וולפסטל
רח' חניתה 83
נוה שאנן
חיפה 3244620

שלום רב,

ביום הזיכרון לשואה ולגבורה, החל השנה, אי"ה, ביום חמישי, כ"ז ניסן התשע"ה , 16 באפריל 2015,
יתקיים בטרקלין שאגאל במשכן הכנסת, בשעה 11:00, הטקס המסורתי הממלכתי –"לכל איש יש שם"–
קריאת שמות הנספים בשואה, במעמד נשיא המדינה ובהשתתפות ראש הממשלה, שרים, חברי הכנסת
ואישי ציבור נוספים.

במהלך הטקס ידליקו 6 נציגים נרות זיכרון, במנורת ה"שישה", לזכר ששת מיליוני היהודים שנרצחו
בשואה, ואת נבחרת להיות אחד מהם.

הגורמים בכנסת, המטפלים בטקס (אגף טקסים ואירועים ורכזת הפרויקט "לכל איש יש שם"), יצרו
איתך קשר, לתיאום הפרטים המתבקשים.

בברכה,

חה"כ יולי (יואל) אדלשטיין
יושב-ראש הכנסת

Speaker of the Knesset
Jerusalem, Tuesday, April 14, 2015
28th of Nissan, Year 5775 by the Jewish calendar

To

Mrs. Masha Wolfsthal
Hanita 83 St.
Neve Shaanan
Haifa 32446

Greetings,

In the coming Holocaust Memorial Day, Thursday, April 16, 2015, the annual "Every Person has a Name" state ceremony will be held at the Chagall State Hall in the Knesset at 11:00 AM, and the names of Holocaust victims will be read in the presence of the President, Prime Minister, ministers, members of the Knesset, and other public figures.

In this ceremony, six delegates will light a memorial candle in the "Menorah of the Six", in memory the six million Jews murdered in the Holocaust, and you have been chosen to be one of them.

The event organizers in the Knesset (Department of Events and Ceremonies and the "Every Person has a Name" project coordinator) will be in touch with you for coordination purposes.

Best regards,

MK Yuli (Yoel) Edelstein
Speaker of the Knesset

Forest of the Martyrs

חמשה עצים
ביער קדושי פולין חורשת קמין קושירסק
ניטעו ע
מאשה דרייזן
לזכר נשמות:
זלג, פריידל, משה, דבורה וליבר
דרייזן
שנספו במשטר הדמים הנאצי

Five trees
were planted in the Kamin-Kashyrskyi grove of the Martyrs of Poland forest
By
Masha Drajcen

In the memory of:
Zelig, Freidel, Moshe, Dvora and Lipa Drajcen
who perished under the murderous Nazi regime.

www.ingramcontent.com/pod-product-compliance
Lightning Source LLC
Chambersburg PA
CBHW050359110426
42812CB00006BA/1742